Sunday Drives

Cruising the Back Roads of Amherst and Nelson Counties

Margaret G. Myers
Ann H. Rucker

Leah S. Gibbs

Illustrated by
Gray S. Dodson
Thomasina Metts

First Edition

ISBN: 978-1-938205-01-9
Printed in the United States of America
Published by Blackwell Press, Lynchburg, Virginia

BLACKWELL
PRESS

Blackwell Press
311 Rivermont Avenue
Lynchburg, Virginia 24504
434-528-4665
www.BlackwellPress.net

Hi & Lois © 2012 King Features Syndicate

Dedications

To our husbands,
as always

To our children,
We are grateful that you were able to grow up in such a lovely area
and we thank you for your encouragement on this book

To our grandchildren,
We hope that these counties of Amherst and Nelson
will still be so scenic that you will want to do some cruising
on the back roads.

CONTENTS

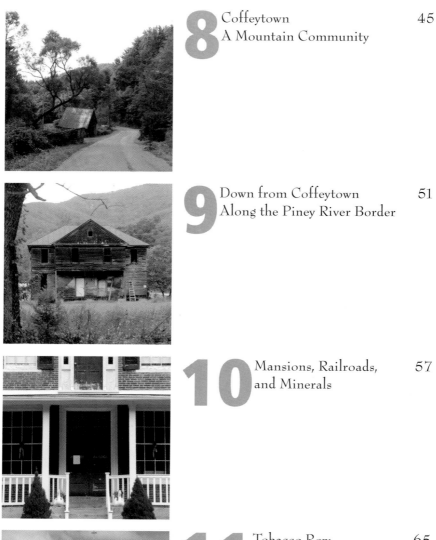

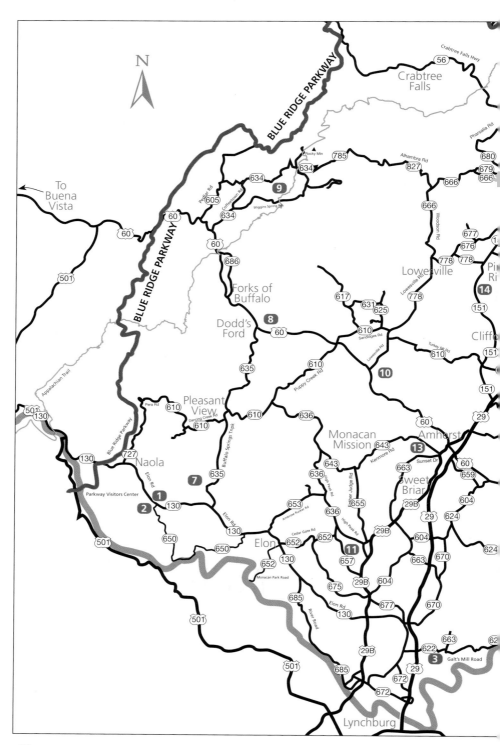

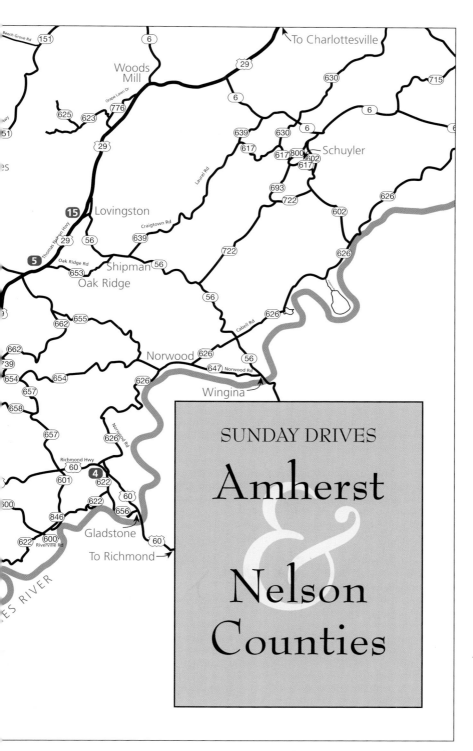

Beech Grove Rd (151)
(6)
To Charlottesville
(29)
(630)
(715)

Woods Mill
(6)
(6)

Grape Lawn Dr
(776)
(630)
(6)

(625) (623)
(639)
(630)
(6)

(29)
(617)
(617) (800) Schuyler
(602)
(617)

Laurel Rd
(693)
(626)

(722)

(15) Lovingston
(602)

Craigtown Rd
(722)

(29) (56)
(639)
(626)

Oak Ridge Rd
Shipman (56)
(626)

(5)
(653)
(56)

Oak Ridge
(56)

(662) (655)
(626)

Cabell Rd
(626)

(662)
(739)
(654) (654)
Norwood (626)
(56)

(657)
(626)
(647) Norwood Rd

(658)
Wingina

(657)
Norwood Rd
(626)

Richmond Hwy
(60)

(4)
(601)
(622)

600
(622)
(60)

(846)
(656)

(622) (600)
Gladstone
(60)

Riverville Rd
To Richmond

ES RIVER

SUNDAY DRIVES

Amherst
&
Nelson
Counties

ix

Sources
which we found useful, and our readers might find interesting—

As longtime residents of these counties, as graduates of Sweet Briar College, and as recent teachers of Virginia and U.S. History, we expected few surprises in writing this book. Who knew?

When we researched the Cabells, for example, we were waylaid for weeks as we delved into *The Cabells and Their Kin*. We finally moved on to topics equally captivating—and about which we had been just as ignorant.

We used very few printed sources, mainly *Heartbeats of Nelson, In the Shadow of Tobacco Row Mountain*, and the county heritage books. We clipped recent newspaper articles and had saved copies of *Lynch's Ferry*.

So many old hard-to-find sources have been digitized that we used the computer for much research. Especially helpful sites were: the Small Manuscripts in the UVa library for the Cabell Family Papers; the Department of Historic Resources for completed applications for historic landmarks; the Virginia Department of Mines and Minerals for mineral resources.

The sources cited are purposely not in proper bibliographic form.

Allen Family of Amherst County, Virginia, The, Charles W. Turner, Ed.

Amherst County, Virginia, I, Heritage Book Committee

Amherst County, Virginia, II, Heritage Book Committee

Atlas of County Boundary Changes in Virginia, 1634-1895, Michael F. Doran

Cabells and Their Kin, The, Alexander Brown

Canal on the James, The, T. Gibson Hobbs, Jr.

Category 5, Ernest Zebrowski

Country Roads, Katherine Tennery and Shirley Scott

Guidebook to Virginia's Historical Markers, A, Department of Historic Resources

Heartbeats of Nelson, Paul Saunders

Indian Island in Amherst County, Peter W. Houck M.D.

Lynch's Ferry, Fall/Winter 1989-1990 ("Queena Stovall," and two other articles by Claudine Weatherford)

Lynch's Ferry, Fall/Winter 2008 ("Books about New Glasgow and Amherst County," Joe Stinnett; "Clifford," Sandi S. Esposito; "Life at Tusculum During the 19th C," Christian Carr; "New Glasgow," Joe Stinnett)

Nelson County, Virginia, Heritage Book Committee

News & Advance, The, and *Amherst New Era-Progress*, "Restoring History." Scott Marshall

Roar of the Heavens, Stefan Bechtel

Acknowledgments

Jessica B. Ward may not know it, but she mentored us by example when she shared her experiences writing her first book, the prize-winning *Food to Die For*. As she was working on her second book, another fund-raiser for the Old City Cemetery, we decided we would like to try writing a fund-raiser for the Amherst and Nelson museums.

At least a decade prior to talking to Jessica Ward at the Downtown Y, one of us was at the Library of Virginia and just happened upon *Country Roads*, a tour guide of Rockbridge County, Virginia, by Katherine Tennery and Shirley Scott. Amherst and Nelson Counties were missing such a guide; maybe we could provide it.

We were also inspired and educated by recent works of local authors: *In the Shadow of Tobacco Row Mountain* by Florence Nixon, *Heartbeats of Nelson* by Paul Saunders, and *Amherst: From Taverns to a Town* by Leah Settle Gibbs and Robert Wimer.

So many people helped us in so many different ways. Lynn Bowling, of Montague, Miller & Co., for instance, donated a number of Amherst/Nelson maps. Our publisher, Nancy Marion, was enthusiastic from day one. Our illustrators, painter Gray Dodson (www.graysdodson.com) and photographer Thomasina Metts (www.photographybythomasina.com), added immensely to the book with their own special talents.

Those who added to our knowledge of Nelson County included David Dodd; Dick and Peggy Whitehead, information about Grace Episcopal Church; Bill Hopkins, information about the Blue Ridge Railroad; and Richard and Dorothy Seaman, information about orchards. In addition, Jimmy and Barbara Wood, Archer Minardi, Digna Gantt, and Paul Heilmann shared information about the Cabells and their homes.

People who helped us with information about Amherst County included Judy Barnes, who told us about orchards and Bethany Church; Holly Mills, who referred us to museum tours, newsletters, and calendars; and Helen Coffey Keith, who told us about growing up in Coffeytown.

A number of people took the time to read over our proofs. Three of our daughters—Sarah Myers, Lucinda Ewing, and Sarah Smith—helped especially with clarity of content. Local historians Florence and Holcomb Nixon, Paul Saunders, and Leah Gibbs shared some of their knowledge. Leah Gibbs actually became a contributing editor by reviewing the entire book and even writing two chapters about Hurricane Camille.

Our husbands, Sammy Myers and Manly Rucker, interested us in Sunday drives in the first place and were willing to answer our many questions about details of Amherst and Nelson history. They, our children, and even some of the grandchildren encouraged us along the way.

Introduction

The Two Counties
and the Purpose of the Book

"Virginia is for lovers," for years the clever slogan of Virginia tourism, stressed the diversity to be found in the Commonwealth. Families packing for the beach, hikers heading to the mountains, and re-enactors gathering on Civil War battlefields . . . all these groups and more can visit the Old Dominion and find just what they want. Amherst and Nelson Counties are also for lovers—lovers of natural beauty—and offer their own wonderful variety. This diversity means that the counties are especially welcoming to those who like to tour the back roads—to take the proverbial Sunday Drives.

Located next to each other in Central Virginia, Amherst and Nelson Counties are practically twins in origin, geography, and population.

Both were once part of Albemarle County until population growth in this area required new county governments closer to the people. In 1761, southern Albemarle became Amherst County, honoring Lord Jeffery Amherst, an officer in the French and Indian War and absentee governor of Virginia. In fewer than fifty years, the rapid growth of Amherst necessitated the formation of yet another county. In 1807, the northern half of Amherst County became Nelson County, named for Thomas Nelson, a signer of the Declaration of Independence from eastern Virginia.

In addition to the counties' origins, their geographies are very much alike. From a bird's eye view, observers could easily see that the Blue Ridge Mountains serve as the counties' western boundary and the James River as their southern and eastern boundaries. Even their individual diamond shapes almost match, as do their square miles. Each county's size is approximately 475 square miles.

The populations of the counties are parallel in demographics—but not in exact numbers. In the two counties, their citizens' average ages, racial percentages, acres owned, and schooling fulfilled look practically the same. What's very much different, however, is the actual population number for each county. Nelson's is a little less than half of Amherst's.

Luckily for each citizen or visitor of whatever age, schooling, property, or race, people in Central Virginia are not yet at the point of the cartoon family shown on page iv. In the cartoon, no undeveloped areas exist in which to picnic or drive. Because of so-called progress, Hi and Lois can only reminisce to their children about Sunday drives and park picnics; their oldest son is even planning to invent a Sunday Drives video game.

Citizens of Amherst and Nelson Counties, however, can still enjoy such live pastimes. Yes, time is precious; yes, gasoline is expensive. Nonetheless, both counties are lovely and well worth anyone's time to cruise a few back roads.

It has been the great pleasure of this book's explorers, writers, editors, publishers, cartographers, and illustrators to compile fifteen such drives as a fundraiser for both counties' historical museums.

HOW TO USE THIS BOOK

Readers may choose chapters in any order.

Each chapter includes the following:

- A preview of the ride,
- The starting point with road names,
- Directions to the starting point from the Amherst Circle at the intersection of Route 60 & Route 29 Business,
- Approximate mileage, not counting any optional side trips,
- Clear directions for the trip itself, and
- Extensive commentary about many points of interest along the way.

HELPFUL REMINDERS

- Set odometer to zero at the starting point. Remember that all mileage is approximate.
- Take along some water and light snacks. Some back roads are way back.
- Be aware of traffic, even on back roads, and prepare to pull over to let non-sightseeing vehicles pass.
- Respect private property.

1
Along the James River:
A Virginia Byway and an
All-American Road

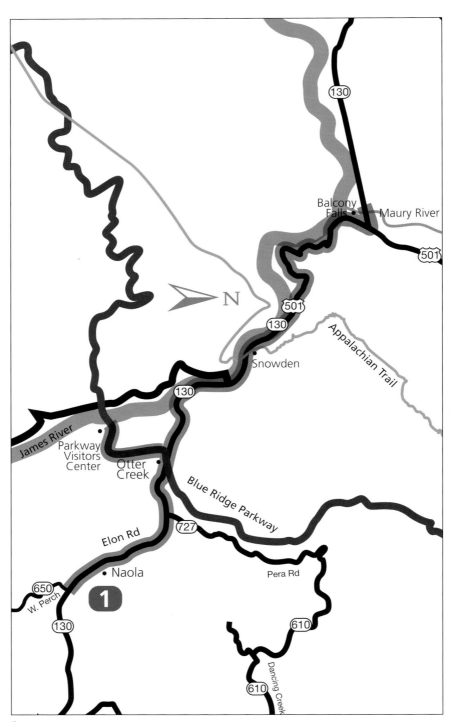

1

Along the James River: A Virginia Byway and an All-American Road

PREVIEW

Elon Road (Rt. 130) is currently Amherst County's only official state scenic highway, or Virginia Byway. The Blue Ridge Parkway is the county's only national scenic highway, or All-American Road. Appropriately, Drive #1 consists of only these two roads as they follow the James River through a gap in the Blue Ridge Mountains—first upriver, then back downriver. Trip-takers will see a restored canal lock, the Balcony Falls Rapids, the James River Face Wilderness Area, and Rockbridge County's Maury River as it enters the James.

TOTAL MILES: 17.7

FROM THE AMHERST CIRCLE:

Take Amherst Highway (Business 29) south for 10 miles, then go west on Elon Road (Rt. 130) for 13 miles.

MILES/DIRECTIONS	COMMENTARY
STARTING POINT This trip begins at the corner of Elon Road (Rt.130) and West Perch Road (Rt. 650). Head straight west on Elon Road (Rt. 130).	
0.9	The Naola sign on the left shows where Floyd's Store and its post office anchored the community.
2.6	A private campground, Wildwood, is open all year. It has a fishing lake and is popular with locals and out-of-towners alike.

3.9
OPTIONAL
STOP
Turn right into the Parkway entrance. At the stop sign, turn left and go south for 2.0 miles. On the left is the James River activity area. Pull in and park.

The Blue Ridge Parkway, recognized by the United States as an All-American Road, was built in the 1930s as a CCC (Civilian Conservation Corps) project to put young men to work during the Great Depression. The Corps members, ages 18 to 25, lived in government camps (one was nearby) and were required to send part of their pay home to their parents. The road actually begins in North Carolina and, after 469 miles, ends near Afton, Virginia.

6.0
When ready to leave the parking lot, turn right. Retrace the route on the Parkway going 2.0 miles north and exit to the right to return to Rt. 130 west.

This stop on the Parkway, directly on the James River at Milepost 63, has much to offer. Picnic tables abound. During the summer, a manned information center is open. Hikers can take a marked trail of trees. History buffs can take a pedestrian bridge across the James River and examine an old lock from the James River-Kanawha Canal.

The canal never officially reached the investors' goal of a canal along and between the James River and the Kanawha River. Their dream was to connect the Atlantic Ocean and the U.S. interior as the famous Erie Canal did. Virginia's canal, nonetheless, provided years of successful water transportation. When the United States entered the railroad age in the middle- to late-19th c., train tracks were much cheaper and quicker than canals to build. In the East especially, tracks were often laid on any canal towpaths available.

8.4

On the right is an entrance to some public ATV trails. Such activities are allowed as recreation, one of the approved uses of national forest land.

11.2
Lee-Jackson Highway (Rt. 501) enters from the left to join Rt. 130.

Keep going straight.

Several dams and small power plants are along the James River. The largest and most recently updated is the Bedford Hydro Plant located here near the 501 bridge.

The Lee-Jackson Highway is named for two Confederate generals, Robert E. Lee and Thomas "Stonewall" Jackson. Route 501 leads to Lexington where both leaders are buried.

Jackson, a math professor at VMI before the Civil War, was mistakenly shot by his own men; when he died, he was brought back to Lexington.

Lee, who had relied strongly on Jackson, survived the war. After the surrender, he accepted the presidency of Washington College in Lexington. Upon his death three years later, he was buried at what's now Lee Chapel on campus.

For the next few miles are some breathtaking views of the James River on the left and some rock outcroppings on the right. Drive as slowly as traffic will allow in order to appreciate these views and perhaps stop at an overlook or two. The return is by the same route.

11.8

A public boat landing is on the right. People in tubing parties are encouraged to exit the river here, not earlier, thus avoiding any railroad tracks.

11.9
OPTIONAL STOP

On the left is where the Appalachian Trail crosses the James River. If desired, pull into the public parking lot and walk out on the bridge (an old railroad trestle) for a close-up view of the river. A train might come along on the newer track and make the stop complete.

A small sign on the right indicates the community of Snowden. Williams' Store, a center for boaters (even water skiers) and hikers, burned in the 1950s. A replacement store, now closed, and several houses are all that remain.

13.1
OPTIONAL STOP

On the left is a large, shady picnic area with a spacious gravel parking lot.

**15.6
OPTIONAL
STOP**

Slow down at the blue Virginia Byway sign, then pull carefully to the left onto a gravel overlook which has no guard rail. The view here includes the Balcony Falls rapids, where the river level drops steeply and quickly within a fairly short space.

The steep mountain face across the James River is in Bedford County, but is federal government property run by the National Park Service. The official name is the James River Face Wilderness Area.

Routes 130 and 501 now crest the Blue Ridge Mountains, thus crossing into Rockbridge County from Amherst County.

17.0

On the left, a small pullover provides a view of the Maury River entering the James River. The Maury is named after Matthew Fontaine Maury, a famous oceanographer nicknamed "Pathfinder of the Seas." He was truly a fascinating scholar, teacher, and adventurer.

17.7
To return, follow Rt. 130/ Rt. 501 across the mountains, then continue east on Rt. 130 after Rt. 501 crosses the James. The trip began at the corner of Rt. 130 and Rt. 650.

It's almost the end of the drive and time to turn around and return to the starting point. Those who want to do so immediately should turn around here at the bridge and return to the starting point.

OR

Those who would like to stretch their legs and maybe get a snack can do so here in the town of Glasgow, which has food, fuel, and even a playground.

**OPTIONAL
LOOP**
Cross the bridge over the Maury River and enter Glasgow, turn left on the first road and go about one-half mile to the dead-end. To leave, exit the parking lot and return to the starting point.

This dead-end road provides a close-up view of the Maury entering the James. It is also a spot for boaters to launch or haul their boats.

2

Three Routes
to the James River
from Elon Road

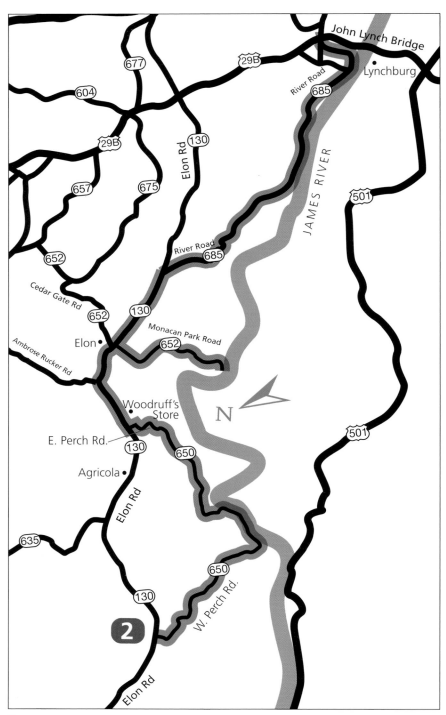

2
Three Routes to the James River from Elon Road

PREVIEW

Drive #1 provided plenty of views of the James River, but mostly aerial views. Elon Road has several other routes to the river. The Perch Road loop is the most rustic and has the closest views of the river. Monacan Park Road, on the other hand, passes modern subdivisions and ends with a playground and public boat ramp in a nicely-maintained waterfront park. Finally, although River Road is also residential, it has wonderful views of stately old houses (one supposedly haunted), deep gorges, a dangerous bridge and, most of all, the river!

TOTAL MILES: 25

FROM THE AMHERST CIRCLE:

From the circle, go south on the Amherst Highway (Business 29) for about 10 miles, then turn right onto Elon Road (Rt. 130) for 13 miles. Turn left onto West Perch Road (Rt. 650).

MILES/DIRECTIONS	COMMENTARY
STARTING POINT Intersection of Elon Road and West Perch Road (Rt. 650).	
0.0 Start down West Perch Road and remain on it for almost 8 miles. In less than a mile there is a fork in the road. Go left to stay on West Perch.	The road loops down to the river, changes its name from West Perch to East Perch and returns to Elon Road.

MILES/DIRECTIONS	COMMENTARY
1.9	Green Valley Meat Processing, a long-time community business, has upgraded its facility to sell to the public through retail stores. This change fits in with the popularity of the local foods movement.
3.0	As the road nears the river it becomes steeper and is no longer paved.
3.5 The road name is now East Perch (Rt. 650).	A popular ferry used to be here. Some folks still tell tales of horses losing their footing and being cut loose from wagons in order to save the cargo.
4.5	At this bridge, the Pedlar River is entering the James River. Nearby is a dam. This area has been flooded, time and again, so much so that some neighbors have had to move their houses to higher ground. Bald eagles have been spotted in this vicinity, usually at the top of the tallest trees.
5.0	The Pedlar River is at the bottom of the deep gorge on the left. The paved road surface returns as do a few houses. Among the new houses are a few older farm houses, such as "Turkey Hill."
7.7	Chestnut Grove Baptist Church, on the left, was founded just after the Civil War in 1866. Twenty years later the congregation moved into the current building.
7.9 At the stop sign marking the end of East Perch Road (Rt. 650), turn right onto Elon Road (Rt. 130).	Woodruff's Store is on the right. For years this landmark was a traditional country store. The new generation has modernized it into a cafe known for its homemade pies.
Drive about 2 miles to the intersection of Elon Road (Rt. 130) and Monacan Park Road (Rt. 676) in the village of Elon.	

MILES/DIRECTIONS	COMMENTARY
10.0 Turn right onto Monacan Park Road.	On the right is Country Corner Market, a local landmark formerly known as Fosters' Store. It and Campbell's Food Store offer food and fuel. CCM's specialties are fresh meat, fried chicken, and salad fixings.
Follow this road 2.6 miles to the James River and Monacan Park.	Monacan Park was built and named by APCO and is maintained by the county. The park offers a playground, a boat launch, picnic tables, and restrooms.
12.6 After leaving the park, take Monacan Park Road (Rt. 676) back to Elon Road (Rt. 130).	
15.2 At the stop sign, turn right on Elon Road (Rt. 130).	East of Elon, a few traditional farm houses stand among the newer homes. On the left, for example, are two of these late-18th c. homes. The second of these was for years the site of annual lawn parties sponsored by the American Legion. Many folks can still remember when Senator John Warner and his wife, movie star Elizabeth Taylor, attended a picnic here.
16.1	On the right in the distance is "The Wigwam," home of the late Queena Stovall, nationally-known late-20th c. folk artist. Her paintings offer a glimpse into everyday life in the Elon area. Prints are still available locally.
	At the beginning of her career, when her family was grown and she was in her sixties, she went to Lynchburg to take an art class. On the first day, the instructor told her to go home—that taking a class might ruin her natural talent.
	Some of her paintings are entitled *March Fury*, *Cabin at Triple Oaks*, *Family Prayers*, and *Making Sorghum Molasses*.
	The huge field in front of her house was for years a race track used for training horses.
17.2 At the intersection of Elon Road (Rt. 130) and River Road (Rt. 685), turn right.	Typical of what is happening seemingly everywhere, a large tract of land has been cut into smaller lots for a subdivision. Amherst County has a zoning ordinance, but currently it is not very restrictive.

MILES/DIRECTIONS	COMMENTARY
18.8	An old log house is on the right.
	As the road curves down towards the river, two late-18th c. farm houses come into view on the left.
20.4	The railroad crossing may seem totally harmless, but look to the left and right to see the great trestles, one crossing Harris Creek and one crossing the James River. Unfortunately, the latter has all too often proved to be a deadly temptation to thrill seekers.
22.0	On the right, another well-kept old house is high on a hill between Harris Creek and the James River. Because rivers were the highways of the early days, this house likely served as a trading center.
22.4	Also on the river is local landmark Red and Dot's, run by the same family for over fifty years. Originally a river recreation center and still a source of vine-ripe tomatoes, the store has recently been remodeled to include a deli known for its half-pound hamburgers.
23.6	On the right is Scott's Dam. A mill was here at one time, but burned. People like to fish along here, but swimming can be very hazardous. Deaths have occurred.
	In earlier times several foundries existed in the area. Then as now, Lynchburg's economic diversity has saved it from dependence on just one industry. Plenty of county workers commute daily to their Lynchburg jobs.
24.0 Drive #2 ends as River Road goes under the "new bridge" and veers left up the hill back to Rt. 29 Business.	Return to the Amherst Circle via Rt. 29 Business North

3

Amherst County's Eastern Boundary:

Riding Along the Mighty James as it Flows Northeast

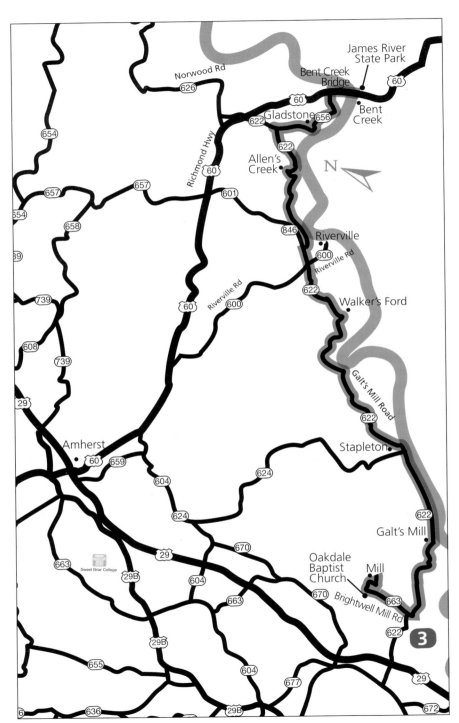

3

Amherst County's Eastern Boundary: Riding Along the Mighty James as it Flows Northeast

PREVIEW

The first four drives in this book focus on the James River, which forms the southern border of Amherst County and the eastern border of both Amherst and Nelson Counties. The first drive is in the mountains, so most views of the river are almost aerial views. The second drive gives three close but short views of the river. Today's drive, #3, basically follows the river on its level, though sometimes the railroad blocks the view. The main difference in the river itself on this drive is that the river has turned and is now flowing northeast.

Today's drive includes Brightwell's Mill and the formerly bustling James River communities from Galt's Mill to Gladstone, almost entirely along Rt. 622. Even though it is on the scenic Virginia map, it is not officially listed.

TOTAL MILES: ABOUT 23

FROM THE AMHERST CIRCLE:

Drive to Madison Heights on South Amherst Highway (Rt. 29 Business) and turn left at the CVS onto Seminole Drive (Rt. 681). When Rt. 681 ends, turn left on Old Wright Shop Road (Rt. 833). When Rt. 833 ends, turn left again on Wright Shop Road (Rt. 622). Turn right on Galt's Mill Road (Rt. 622); continue until reaching Oakdale Baptist Church at the corner of Brightwell's Mill Road (Rt. 663).

MILES/DIRECTIONS	COMMENTARY
STARTING POINT Oakdale Baptist Church—Galt's Mill Road (Rt. 622) & Brightwell's Mill Road (Rt. 663)	An outdoor revival in 1906 led to a number of baptisms and the founding of Oakdale Baptist Church. The building itself was dedicated a few years later. The building has been improved and the congregation has continued to grow over the years.

15

MILES/DIRECTIONS	COMMENTARY
1.1 Drive east on Brightwell's Mill Road. (Rt. 663)	Brightwell's Mill, though in disrepair, is nonetheless still imposing. Built in the 1800s, it was rebuilt after a flash flood in the 1940s. The Brightwell family is hoping to put the mill on the historic landmark list. Family members have already begun to restore it and would be glad for assistance on this wonderful project.
2.3 Return to Oakdale Baptist Church. Make a sharp left onto Galt's Mill Road (Rt. 622).	This road follows the James River until reaching Nelson County.
4.8	After two and a half miles of curvy roads and dense woods, a pleasant surprise awaits: a wide-open view of the James River and the railroad running beside it. As in many other places, railroads laid their tracks on canal tow-paths, thus putting the railroads right next to the river. This area is called Galt's Mill. The old house and its outbuildings are listed on the National Registry as the "Galt's Mill Complex."
11.5 Continue following Galt's Mill Road (Rt. 622).	After Galt's Mill, the road, the river, and the railroad tracks pass near or through the formerly busy communities of Stapleton, Walker's Ford, Riverville, Allen's Creek, and Gladstone. Each had a store/post office plus a few other amenities such as a school, a church, or railroad station. Between these old communities are some large new farms, for instance "Townley IV Farms."
13.0	Just before the entrance to the paper mill at Riverville is another large farm, "Edge Hill." A lovely old brick home currently listed as a national landmark, it was once used as a hospitality center for visitors to the mill. The mill no longer owns the house.
13.9	At Riverville is the entrance to Greif Brothers Paper Mill, formerly Virginia Fiber, a large employer in Amherst County since the 1980s.

16

14.6
OPTIONAL
DETOUR
Turn right on
Riverville Road (Rt.
600) and go to the
end of the road at
the railroad tracks.

Return to Rt. 622.
The name of the
road soon changes
to Piedmont Road,
then to Allen's Creek
Road.

On the right is the old Riverville Store, currently a residence. On the left is a large rocky field. During the 1950s, at the height of the Cold War between the U.S. and the Soviet Union, this area held a huge stockpile of manganese, a mineral necessary in the production of steel. Local observers say the pile was like a mountain and a fairly recent newspaper article claimed it held 300,000 tons.

When Cold War fears receded, the government removed its strategic stockpile by hiring drivers with dump trucks to fill train cars.

15.0
Continue on Allen's
Creek Road (Rt. 622)
as it turns right.

17.6
Notice that the drive
has crossed into
Nelson County.

Driving this close to the railroad track is probably a little frightening when the train comes by.

18.3
Beware of a
surprisingly sharp
curve to the right.

18.9
Turn right onto
Gladstone Road (Rt.
656).

This road leads first to Allen's Creek, then to Gladstone, an old railroad town in Nelson County. Gladstone Memorial Church is still active. The town is nowhere as busy as it was when the railroad was the primary freight carrier. The many rows of tracks and the now-empty store and Masonic Hall indicate the town's formerly thriving status.

21.2
Turn right onto
Richmond Highway
(Rt. 60). Go straight
east until you cross
the river at Bent
Creek.

This large bridge was built in the1960s over the James River, a border here between Nelson and Appomattox Counties.

On the north side of Rt. 60 is the entrance to James River State Park. It's worth a tour either now or some other time. The land for the park included the former site of a Cabell home, "Green Hill."

END OF DRIVE
#3
Turn around,
and return to the
Amherst traffic circle
by heading west on
Richmond Highway
(Rt. 60)

OR
Go ahead and start
Drive # 4 by heading
west, then turning
right off Richmond
Highway (Rt. 60)
onto the Norwood
Road (Rt. 626).

4

Cabell Territory— Along the James River in Nelson County

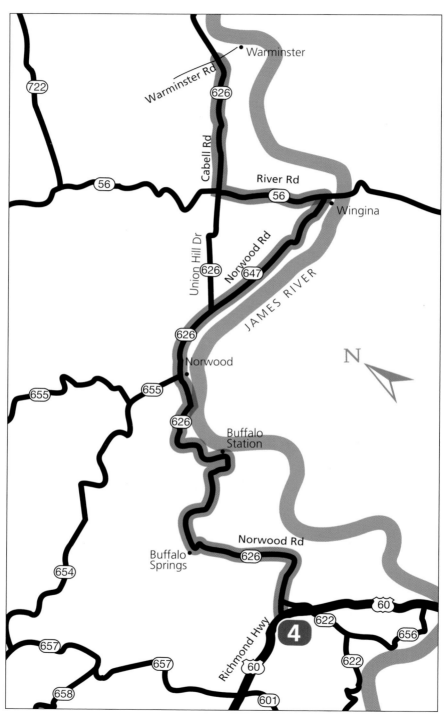

4

Cabell Territory—
Along the James River
in Nelson County

PREVIEW

Today's drive is again along the James River, but this time solely in Nelson County as the James continues flowing northeast. This particular area could be called Cabell Territory as the Cabell family began its dynasty here. In the early 1700s, Dr. William Cabell claimed thousands of acres of the yet-unsettled bottom land on the James River. Dr. Cabell's sons and grandsons, like Dr. Cabell, became successful merchants, developers, and professionals. The Cabell women were capable rulers of their traditional domains…and sometimes of nontraditional ones also. When Dr. William Cabell had to return to England for several years, for instance, Elizabeth Cabell increased their land holdings almost sevenfold.

Over the years, many of the Cabells built lovely large homes along or near the river. They also served their governments—first local and colonial, and eventually their state and national governments. Some even named or renamed their homes to reflect their support of the new United States; examples are "Union Hill" and "Liberty Hall."

TOTAL MILES: 22

FROM THE AMHERST CIRCLE:

From the Amherst Circle go east on Richmond Highway (Rt. 60). Go 11.3 miles until reaching the Norwood Road (Rt. 626) on the left.

MILES/DIRECTIONS	COMMENTARY
STARTING POINT The corner of Richmond Highway (Rt. 60) and Norwood Road (Rt. 626)	
0.0 Follow Norwood Road (Rt. 626).	

0.3 – 0.8	In the area near Second Mineral Springs Baptist Church and Mineral Springs Baptist Church was once a thriving spa and hotel, "Buffalo Springs," which burned in the early 20th century. Nearby, on the James River, was Buffalo Station, where the train stopped to bring visitors to the hotel. This spa was so successful that it bottled its own water, labeled "Buffalo Mineral Water," and claimed that "physicians… in the United States and in Europe… have recommended it to their patients." Amherst County also had a resort by the same name, described in Drive #7. Spas were popular in the 19th century as people believed that "taking the waters" (usually drinking or occasionally bathing in mineral water) was very healthful.
8.2	Norwood, where the Tye River flows into the James, was a natural spot for a trade center. It had everything it needed: the James River, the James River-Kanawha Canal, and eventually, the railroad, plus the Cabells with their mercantile expertise. In the early 19th century, one role the town played was to serve as a weigh station for tobacco, still an important cash crop. Besides coming to town to have their tobacco weighed, farmers needed to come to the mill to have their corn ground. Today in the Norwood area, remains can be found of one of the Cabells' mills—one of seven they owned.
8.6	In the distance is a large metal railroad bridge crossing the Tye River as it flows into the James. This bridge and its predecessors were very important to commerce. If threatened, as in the Civil War during the Battle of Lynchburg, it was defended; if damaged, as a century later during Hurricane Camille, it would be repaired.

Besides its importance as a trade center, the Norwood area is an architectural wonderland of homes built by members of the Cabell family. Within a dozen miles of here are or were at least a dozen of the almost forty homes built by the Cabells.

The names of these nearby houses are as follows: "Oak Ridge," "Inglewood," "Fork Field," "Montezuma," "Norwood," "Union Hill," "Colleton," "Rock Cliff," "Soldier's Joy," |

"Bon Aire," "Liberty Hall," and "Edgewood," according to the Cabell Foundation maps. Some, such as "Rock Cliff" and the "Edgewood" outbuildings are still owned by direct Cabell descendants.

A few houses, such as "Montezuma" and "Bon Aire," can be spotted from the road. Because of concerns for the privacy of the owners, this particular drive will not include a tour of individual Cabell houses. A wealth of information is available in print and online about the fascinating and prolific Cabell family. Also, two other drives will show close-up views and possible tours of Cabell homes. Drive #5 focuses on "Oak Ridge" and Drive #10 includes "Mountain View" and "Winton," both in the Clifford area.

Tour-takers familiar with the Lynchburg area just south of Amherst County probably have heard of Cabell Street and its landmark house built for a Dr. Cabell. The name of the house, "Point of Honor," supposedly came from a duel which took place there. That particular house is currently part of the city museum system and is open to the public.

Those who wish to pursue further study about the Cabells and their homes will find that every Cabell house has an interesting history. For instance, "Soldier's Joy" was named when a Cabell son came home safely from the Revolutionary War. The ballroom of the same house is no longer attached to the house—a few decades ago, it was dismantled and sold to a museum. By then, hardly anyone entertained in a manner to need a ballroom. Prior to its sale, that particular ballroom was being used to store hay. Occasionally, an entire house would gain a new use. From about 1860 to 1890, "Norwood," for instance, became a preparatory school for the University of Virginia. Later, in the 20th century, it served as a dance school and summer camp.

Fire was a constant danger to early homes; those of the Cabells were no exception. "Liberty Hall," burned in 1895 and "Edgewood" in 1955.

MILES/DIRECTIONS	COMMENTARY
8.8 Enjoy almost 5 miles of straight and flat driving from here to Wingina.	On the right is a former church, now privately owned. Nearby, a marker refers to this area as the boyhood home of the Rev. William Goodwin. While he served at Bruton Parish Church, his ideas of restoring Colonial Williamsburg interested John D. Rockefeller, who turned the dreams into reality. Despite its current rural simplicity, Norwood's former leadership role during the colonial, revolutionary, and early national eras has led some to suggest applying for state historical status.
13.6 Continue on Norwood Rd. (Rt. 626) until the intersection with River Road (Rt. 56).	At the end of Norwood Road, at the intersection with River Road (Rt. 56), the old store on the left houses the post office for Wingina, 24599. The post office is still functioning, but the store is not.
13.6 Turn left onto River Road (Rt. 56 west)	
15.9 Turn right on Cabell Rd. (Rt. 626) and go about 3 miles to Warminister Road. Turn around here.	On the left is Warminster Rd., all that remains of a thriving village of the same name. Dr. Cabell named the village after his home in England.
19.3 Return to River Road (Rt. 56). This is the end of Drive #4.	

TWO CHOICES FOR THE RETURN TO THE TRAFFIC CIRCLE:

Turn left on River Road (Rt. 56), right on the Norwood Road (Rt. 626) , and right on Richmond Highway (Rt.60) to enjoy the tour in reverse.

OR

For a quicker return,
turn right on River Road (Rt. 56), go about 10 miles to turn left on Lovington's Front St. Turn left again at the stop light onto Thomas Nelson Highway (Rt. 29) and go south until reaching the Amherst traffic circle .

5

The Cabells and the Waltons

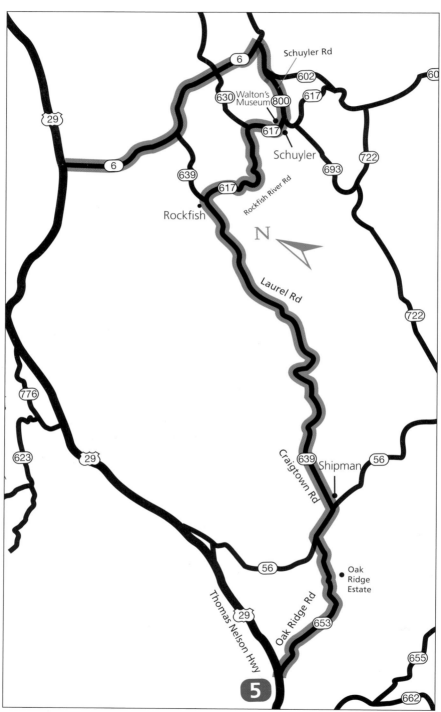

5

The Cabells and the Waltons

PREVIEW:
Mentioned in Drive #4 were the successful Cabell families and their homes. In today's drive, the focus is on just two Nelson County families and their homes, one in Oak Ridge and one in Schuyler. The two families are almost opposite in so many ways, from farm size to family size, from their era to their fame, from truth to fiction. Might they, however, be more similar than different?

TOTAL MILES: ABOUT 20

FROM THE AMHERST CIRCLE:

Go approximately fifteen miles north to the intersection of Thomas Nelson Highway (Rt. 29) and Oak Ridge Drive (Rt. 653).

MILES/DIRECTIONS	COMMENTARY
STARTING POINT Intersection of Thomas Nelson Highway (Rt. 29) and Oak Ridge Rd. (Rt. 653).	At this spot are two historical markers, one for the birth place of William Cabell Rives and the other for his home, "Oak Ridge," which was built by his father, Robert Rives.
	In 1901, Thomas Fortune Ryan, a successful financier originally from the area, bought the estate. His life, with its "poor boy makes good" plot, sounds as if it should be a story by Horatio Alger. Ryan added to "Oak Ridge" and transformed the grounds into a self-sufficient community.
Turn right onto Oak Ridge Rd. (Rt. 653).	
	The almost 5,000-acre estate is currently owned by the Hollands, who have spent several years restoring the house. They continue to make improvements on the grounds and outbuildings.
0.5	Trinity Episcopal Church was once known as Rives' Church, after Robert Rives built it in the 1830s. At that time, it was a community church serving Methodists, Baptists, and Episcopalians. Both whites and blacks, free and slave, attended.
	Across the road at the corner stands a statue of Atlas holding the earth. The United States is painted in red, white, and blue and a reference is made to 9/11/01.

2.4

Stay on Oak Ridge Rd. (Rt. 653) until an open gate and Oak Ridge sign indicate the entrance to the house.

If you are planning to tour, pull into the driveway and continue to the house.

"Oak Ridge" is a fine colonial home built in 1802 by Robert Rives and his wife, Margaret Cabell Rives. Currently, the house is open to visitors for a fee from spring to fall during the middle of the week. For updates, check the "Oak Ridge" website, www.oakridgeestate.com.

Upon leaving the Oak Ridge driveway, continue on Oak Ridge Rd. (Rt. 653). Follow this road until reaching the intersection with River Road (Rt. 56) in Shipman.

As tourists pass the carriage house and leave the grandeur of the "Oak Ridge" estate and the lives of the Cabells, they return to what many people might call 21st c. normality.

A family superficially different from the Cabells, and probably much better known nowadays than the Cabells, is the Walton family of literary, film, and television fame. Particularly in the 1970s, "The Waltons" television series had a loyal following among people of all ages.

Earl Hamner, Jr., wrote about his growing-up years in the small rural community of Schuyler, slightly fictionalizing himself as "John Boy" Walton. The Waltons were a hard-working, patriotic, and loving family living through the Great Depression and World War II. Because of Hamner's skill as an author and a playwright, the Library of Virginia recently honored him for his life's work.

Head toward Schuyler, home of the real-life Hamners and fictional Waltons, by way of Shipman.

4.2

Turn right onto River Road (Rt. 56).

Shipman was home to Peter Cartwright, who was neither a Hamner nor a Cabell. He was born just east of Shipman in 1785, when this area was still part of Amherst County. In the early 19th century, as part of the 2nd Great Awakening, he led revivals on the frontier. Later, as a circuit rider in the Midwest, he helped develop Methodism. He was also active in Illinois politics, defeating Abraham Lincoln in one election and defeated by Lincoln in another. In his honor, at least one local Methodist congregation has a Sunday School class called the "Peter Cartwright Class."

MILES/DIRECTIONS	COMMENTARY
Immediately before the railroad tracks, turn left onto Craigtown Road (Rt. 639).	
Keep going straight for about 1.5 miles, then. . . look out! A sharp curve precedes a railroad track, another follows.	This area is listed on maps as Elma. The name of Rt. 639 changes from Craigtown Road to Laurel Road.
8.3 Turn right onto Rockfish River Road (Rt. 617)	Just recently, Virginia named Schuyler Rd. (Rt. 800) and Rockfish River Rd. (Rt. 617) as official scenic byways. Besides having great views, the roads are also significant because they lead to Schuyler, the setting of "The Waltons," as previously mentioned.
12.1	The very small town of Schuyler has dedicated itself to Earl Hamner, Jr., and the Walton series: the old elementary school is the site of the Walton's Mountain Museum; the old store sells memorabilia; the Hamners' actual house is open for tours. Further information is at www.waltonsmuseum.org.
12.4 Continue on Rockfish River Rd. (Rt. 617) uphill past the museum and the rest of Schuyler. Turn left on Schuyler Rd. (Rt. 800).	Past Schuyler on the right is the Alberene Soapstone Plant. A long-time business in the area, the plant once employed several hundred people. Before moving to Nelson County, the Alberene Soapstone Plant had its business in nearby Albemarle County. The plant had to leave its namesake town because it had depleted the vein of soapstone in that area. Soapstone, a particularly dense material, can hold in heat or liquid. Soapstone stoves let the heat out slowly and evenly; soapstone countertops, sinks and tiles repel both heat and liquids. Some say that soapstone operating tables were once considered the best. The Nelson Plant is currently open, but on a much smaller scale.

29

People taking Drive #5 were left with a question when they finished reading the Preview. As they head away from the Schuyler area they might think again of the contrasts between the families of "Oak Ridge" and Schuyler.

With over thirty homes near the James River, the Cabells formed a land-holding elite, often providing formal political leadership.

The fictional Waltons were small landholders, the proverbial "salt of the earth," who provided informal leadership within their families and communities.

More important, however, might be what the two families had in common. Although the Cabells and the Waltons lived in different eras and were in some ways opposites, both exemplified the natural leadership the U.S. needed—and still needs.

14.6
Turn left onto Irish Road (Rt. 6) and follow it for almost 6 miles.

20.3
At the intersection of Irish Road (Rt. 6) with Thomas Nelson Highway (Rt. 29) Drive #5 ends.

TO RETURN TO THE CIRCLE
Turn left on Thomas Nelson Highway (Rt. 29) south.

Route 29 South passes through Woods Mill and the outskirts of Lovingston, the county seat. Another chapter in this book covers in detail the effects of Hurricane Camille on these communities.

Another landmark on the way back to the circle is "Oakland," an early 19th c. home, tavern, and stagecoach stop. Now, it serves as the Nelson County Museum of History. The museum focuses on 20th c. local history, including Hurricane Camille and its aftermath. Currently the museum is open only on weekends, with further information at www.nelsonhistorical.com.

6
Two + One = Three
Special Nelson County Roads

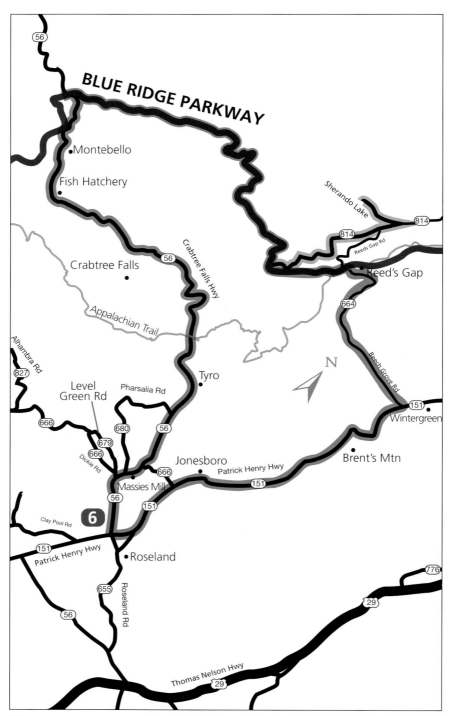

BLUE RIDGE PARKWAY

•Montebello

•Fish Hatchery

Sherando Lake

814

814

Reeds Gap Rd

Crabtree Falls Hwy

Crabtree Falls

56

Reed's Gap

Appalachian Trail

664

Alhambra Rd

827

Level Green Rd

Pharsalia Rd

Tyro

N

Beech Grove Rd

151

Wintergreen

666

680

56

679

666

Dickie Rd

Jonesboro

666

Patrick Henry Hwy

151

Brent's Mtn

Massies Mill

56

151

6

Clay Pool Rd

151

Patrick Henry Hwy

•Roseland

776

655

Roseland Rd

29

56

Thomas Nelson Hwy

29

6

Two + One = Three
Special Nelson County Roads

PREVIEW:
Three officially scenic roads are on the agenda of today's drive—two verified by the Commonwealth of Virginia as Virginia Byways and one verified by the United States as an All-American Road. Beginning straight and flat along the wide Tye River, Virginia Byway Crabtree Falls Highway (Rt. 56) curves more as it rises through the mountains. The All-American Blue Ridge Parkway goes along the top ridges of the mountains in long, sweeping curves which provide panoramic views. On the return, the Virginia Byway is the Patrick Henry Highway (Rt. 151).

TOTAL MILES: 38

FROM THE AMHERST CIRCLE:
Take North Amherst Highway (Rt. 29 Business, then Rt. 29). In 2.5 miles turn left onto Patrick Henry Highway (Rt. 151). In 11.3 miles turn left onto Crabtree Falls Highway (Rt. 56).

MILES/DIRECTIONS	COMMENTARY
STARTING POINT Intersection of Patrick Henry Highway (Rt. 151) and Crabtree Falls Highway (Rt. 56).	Both these roads are Virginia Byways—two of Nelson County's six.
0 Travel west on Crabtree Falls Highway (Rt. 56).	Under various names, Route 56 traverses almost the entire county of Nelson; it starts at Wingina on the James River as River Road and ends at the Blue Ridge Parkway in the mountains. Today's portion of Rt. 56 passes through three small communities, the first being Massies Mill.

1.3 On the left is Fleetwood Community Center. Fleetwood started as a high school, was accredited by the state, then continued solely as an elementary school. This change occurred in the 1950s when local high schools merged into district high schools. Currently, as many counties do, Nelson uses large consolidated schools rather than small community schools; the high school and middle school are together, and an elementary school is at each end of the county.

1.7 On the right is a stone memorial to those who lost their lives or property as a result of Hurricane Camille. The memorial is set in a small garden.

1.8 According to a nearby historical marker, soon after the Revolutionary War, Major Thomas Massie acquired several thousand acres. He then settled his family at nearby Level Green Plantation and built a much-needed mill; thus, the area became known as Massies Mill.

1.9 On the right is Grace Episcopal Church, built in the late 1880s. The land was donated by the Massie family and built by members of the community.

When Hurricane Camille came through Nelson County in 1969, it seriously damaged Massies Mill and other similarly situated riverside communities. The Grace Episcopal congregation feels especially blessed that two maple trees in the churchyard diverted debris from the flood waters, thus saving the church from total destruction.

The last two drives in this book are solely about the deadly hurricane of 1969.

Soon on the left is the modern Massies Mill Presbyterian Church. Originally constructed just a few years after Grace Episcopal, the Presbyterian Church was totally destroyed by Hurricane Camille, but was replaced immediately.

All over Nelson County was similar devastation. Generous volunteers from home and away made a great effort to rebuild. Organizations such as the Red Cross and church congregations, including the Mennonites and others, joined individuals for months or even longer. The citizens of Nelson were then and are still grateful for their help.

5.0
OPTIONAL
STOP

Tyro, the second small community, includes Silver Creek-Seaman Packing Shed. Here two long-time Nelson County orchards offer their apples for sale from September to November in their retail room. Other local orchards include Saunders Brothers, Dickie Brothers, Drumheller, Mt. Cove, and Fitzgerald. Nelson and Amherst Counties are fertile regions for growing apples, peaches and more recently grapes.

11.0

Route 56 continues past Tyro toward Crabtree Falls. Here are a dozen or so public lodgings, including a campground. For further information on lodging, check the county website, www. nelsoncounty.com/visit/crabtreefalls/.

11.6
OPTIONAL
STOP

Crabtree Falls Highway brings travelers to one of the highest waterfalls east of the Mississippi. The National Forest System took over the falls in the late 1960s and has built stairs to the top with overlooks along the way. The first overlook is just a few feet up the falls, so this site can be accessed by almost anyone. Adventuresome climbers must remember to stay behind the fences along the trail. More than twenty climbers have been killed in tragic accidents at Crabtree Falls by venturing too close to the stream. Be careful!

MILES/DIRECTIONS	COMMENTARY
14.7 **OPTIONAL** **STOP**	A few miles past Crabtree Falls is the third small community on this drive, Montebello. On the left is the entrance to Montebello State Trout Hatchery, run by the Department of Game and Inland Fisheries to stock creeks and streams east of the Blue Ridge. The public may visit daily from 8:30 to 3:30.
15.1 **OPTIONAL** **STOP**	A little past the hatchery is Montebello Country Store, which offers a nice break before going on the Blue Ridge Parkway. It serves meals, offers plenty of shopping, and is the Montebello post office.
18.1 Turn right to enter the Parkway, then turn right again to go north.	Enjoy the lovely views, some with and some without overlooks.
20.1	Although there is no overlook, the Christmas tree farm on the right is large enough for even the driver to glimpse for a second.
22.2, 23.0, 26.3	Several overlooks are as marked.
29.0 **OPTIONAL** **DETOUR** Leave the parkway at the Love, Va. Exit and take Rt. 814. Go 4.5 miles to Sherando Lake. After an optional sojourn there, return to the parkway via Rt. 814.	Enjoy Sherando Lake, run by the National Park Service. Available activities include wading, swimming, playing volleyball, hiking, and even camping.
31.5 Turn right to leave the Parkway at Reed's Gap. Get on Beech Grove Rd. (Rt. 664).	It's time to leave the Parkway and return to state roads heading back to the Tye River bottom lands (the starting point).

MILES/DIRECTIONS	COMMENTARY
32.6	On the left is an entrance to Wintergreen, a popular ski and golf resort, which has been open to the public since the mid-1970s. The resort has changed hands recently and many upgrades are in store. Check their website for the latest information at www.wintergreenresort.com.
36.0–37.0	Civilization reemerges in the form of gas stations, stores, Beech Grove Christian Church, Devil's Backbone Brewery, and the Ski Barn.
38.0 Turn right on Patrick Henry Highway (Rt. 151).	Beware of hairpin turns on Brent's Mountain.
45.2	On the right is a well-known old church in the area, Jonesboro Baptist Church and its cemetery. The current "Gothic Gospel" style church was completed in 1878, replacing an earlier building.
46.6	Roseland, a widespread community with many cattle farms, fairly new vineyards, and mature orchards, was named for the Rev. Robert Rose.
47.4 Intersection of Rt. 151 & Rt. 56	Back to starting point, and the end of Drive #6
To return to the Amherst Circle, take Rt. 151 to Rt. 29, then Rt. 29 south to the circle.	

7

Three Communities Along Buffalo Springs Turnpike

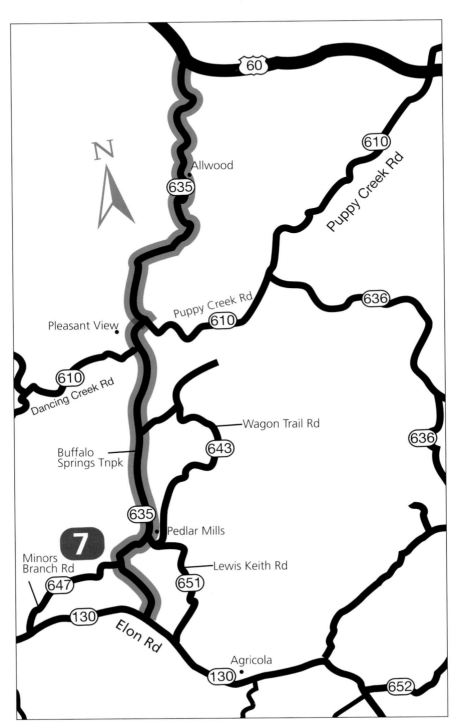

N

60

610

Puppy Creek Rd

Allwood

635

636

Puppy Creek Rd

Pleasant View

610

610

Dancing Creek Rd

Wagon Trail Rd

Buffalo
Springs Tnpk

643

636

635

7

Pedlar Mills

Minors
Branch Rd

647

Lewis Keith Rd

651

130

Elon Rd

Agricola

130

652

7

Three Communities Along Buffalo Springs Turnpike

PREVIEW

Just west of Tobacco Row Mountain, the Buffalo Springs Turnpike (Rt. 635) runs between Elon Road (Rt. 130) and Lexington Highway (Rt. 60). Not too long ago three small, once thriving communities on the road were population and commercial centers for the area. Mills, stores, taverns, post offices, lumber yards, even a resort hotel -- they had it all. The road itself was part of the stage coach highway between the cities of Lexington and Lynchburg. Some evidence of that heyday still exists in various forms. An old tavern is now a nice home, but an abandoned store is deteriorating rapidly.

Today, the automobile has eliminated the need for a post office and a store every mile or so. Nonetheless, these communities aren't total ghost towns, but have changed into a cross between old-fashioned rural communities and modern-day suburbs. Although the buildings and the demographics may have changed somewhat, the gorgeous views remain.

TOTAL MILES: 10.5
FROM THE AMHERST CIRCLE:
Go approximately 10 miles on Rt. 29-S, then about 12 miles west to the intersection of Rt. 130 and Rt. 635.

MILES/DIRECTIONS	COMMENTARY
STARTING POINT The intersection of Elon Road (Rt. 130) and Buffalo Springs Turnpike (Rt. 635)	
0.0 Go north on Buffalo Springs Turnpike (Rt. 635). Stay on this road for the entire trip.	

0.1

The Pedlar River heads to the James River and eventually to the Chesapeake Bay.

A covered bridge crossed the Pedlar River here until it was replaced by the current bridge about 80 years ago. Supposedly no bridge will be needed here after a new bridge replaces the current single-lane bridge over Horsley's Creek and the road is reconfigured.

Several swinging bridges just for pedestrians were also in the area.

1.0

To the left is Minors Branch Road. This road, Minors Branch, and Minors Mountain were named for a local farmer and businessman, Lancelot Minor, who lived nearby during the 19th century. The famous University of Virginia law professor, John B. Minor, for whom a building on the grounds was named, was not Lancelot, but a relative of his.

1.3

The large white house on the left is about 100 years old. Hurricane Camille washed away the other buildings on the place: Pedlar Mills School, a blacksmith shop, and a store.

St. Luke's Church and cemetery are on the left. The Ellis family and others in the community supported the founding of this congregation circa 1800, although this building is not the original building. In the 1830s St. Luke's was built of brick; in the 1870s it was rebuilt using the same brick; the portico was added in the 1920s.

Like those of many other rural churches, St. Luke's numbers dwindled in the late 20th century. At St. Luke's, however, some interested members and friends of St. Luke's have brought the church back to life with weekly services.

The Ellis family mentioned above owned much land in this area. The first 1000 acres came to Captain Charles Ellis as a land grant for war services; in 1754 he and his family moved here. Gradually they added property and eventually owned businesses in both Pedlar Mills and Richmond.

Edgar Allan Poe, foster son of the Richmond business partners of the Ellis family, often came to "Red Hill," the Ellises' brick house on the outskirts of Pedlar Mills.

This home is on the national historic landmark list—only the third from Amherst County to be placed on it.

1.5

Continue going straight through Pedlar Mills on Buffalo Springs Turnpike (Rt. 635).

Currently the community of Pedlar Mills appears to be no more than a few houses where Horsley's Creek joins the Pedlar River. According to a 2010 state survey of historical buildings in Amherst County, however, Pedlar Mills was once a thriving commercial center. According to the researchers, enough artifacts remain to apply to have Pedlar Mills declared a state historic district.

The tavern mentioned in the preview, one of the old buildings restored, was built in 1813. Over the years it served as stagecoach stop, doctor's office and school. One of the swinging bridges mentioned above crossed Horsley's Creek here.

On the right for most of the drive along Buffalo Springs Turnpike, especially between Pedlar Mills and Pleasant View, Tobacco Row Mountain can be seen in all its glory, no matter what the season.

5.3

Continue going straight through Pleasant View on Buffalo Springs Turnpike (Rt. 635).

Pleasant View Elementary School is similar to Temperance Elementary; both are small schools serving the less-populated western part of the county.

Ahead at the three-way intersection of Puppy Creek Road (Rt. 610) and Buffalo Springs Turnpike (Rt. 635) is the actual center of Pleasant View. The large and rambling Pleasant View Store, currently closed, is on the left; New Prospect Baptist Church is on the right. It has been in the same spot since the 1820s and in the same building since the 1840s. The first congregation in this building numbered approximately 200 blacks and 200 whites. The old Pleasant View High School, which was behind the church, made its auditorium available for the church to use as a social hall after the high school closed.

43

MILES/DIRECTIONS	COMMENTARY
5.6	Timothy Baptist Church was built in 1870, just five years after the end of the Civil War. The original white frame building stood for nearly 110 years and then was reconstructed in brick. Next to the church was once the two-room Timothy School; it closed in the 1960s.
8.4	El Bethel Methodist Church, founded in 1837, is the first indication of the Allwood community. Typical of many churches in rural areas, El Bethel no longer has a congregation. Instead, it is supported by the Ruritan Club as a community service. The club and area churches sponsor annual Easter sunrise services here.
9.0 Continue going straight through Allwood on Buffalo Springs Turnpike (Rt. 635).	The Davis Store, a familiar landmark, has been at the center of Allwood since 1950.
10.0 Continue going straight on Buffalo Springs Turnpike (Rt. 635).	Nearby are the remains of the old Buffalo Springs Resort Hotel, for which the road is named. People came to stay in small cabins or the hotel and enjoy the benefits of the sulfur water springs. A visitor once claimed that the water tasted pretty good, but it made the worst coffee he ever tasted. Originally in the early 1800s the resort was just a group of cabins around the springs. Eventually, one of the owners added a hotel which burned and was later replaced. The new hotel had two two-story porches, including a promenade porch. The spring itself was enclosed by a large gazebo. It had a reputation as a quiet place where families were welcomed. One of the last activities held on the hotel grounds was a 100th birthday party for a local gentleman. Around the 1920s, the hotel ceased serving the public.
10.5	The stop sign marks the end of Drive #7. Either turn right on the Amherst-Lexington Highway (Rt. 60) to return to the Amherst Circle in about ten miles, or turn left to begin Trip #8.

8
Coffeytown
A Mountain Community

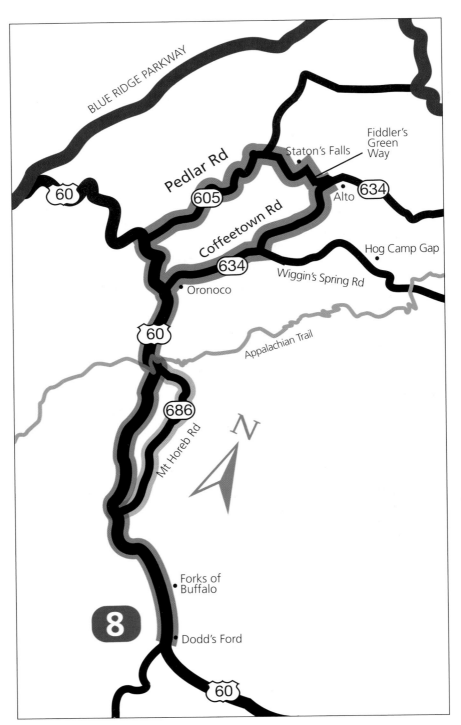

8

Coffeytown
A Mountain Community

PREVIEW:

"Getting there is half the fun," once a slogan for a bus company, is certainly true about the trip to the community of Coffeytown, listed on maps as Alto. Like so many other small communities of the earlier days, Alto centered around a store, a school and a church. The Coffeys, a large family, owned the store and a number of houses in the community. It's no wonder the town became known to most as Coffeytown, just as the road became known as Coffeytown Road. Starting at Dodd's Ford, passing the Forks of Buffalo, heading up Long Mountain—all these and more are part of driving to Coffeytown.

If "getting there is half the fun," then being there must be the other half. Some might not know the latest news from Coffeytown itself: the church has just recently been listed as a state and national historic landmark. Quite a feather in its cap for a small mountain community!

TOTAL MILES: 22
FROM THE AMHERST CIRCLE:
Go west twelve miles on Amherst-Lexington Highway (Rt.60) until reaching the corner of Amherst-Lexington Highway (Rt. 60) and Buffalo Springs Turnpike (Rt. 635).

MILES/DIRECTIONS	COMMENTARY
STARTING POINT At Dodd's Ford, which is at the corner of Amherst-Lexington Highway (Rt. 60) and Buffalo Springs Turnpike (Rt. 635).	Dodd's Ford, a crossing for the Buffalo River, is sometimes called Dodd's Store instead. The store recently burned.
	On the left is Pedlar Volunteer Fire Dept. and Rescue Squad, which raises funds for its work by having Sunday dinners here.

MILES/DIRECTIONS	COMMENTARY
0.7 Continue going straight through Forks of Buffalo on the Amherst-Lexington Highway (Rt. 60).	Forks of Buffalo was once a busy community like the others on the Buffalo Springs Turnpike (Rt. 635). The community store, although still standing, has closed, as has its post office. The mill and cannery have also closed. Many of the families who once worked small mountain farms along the north fork have moved to town.
6.7 Turn right on Pedlar River Road (Rt. 605).	This area is called Oronoco, which is also the name of a certain type of tobacco. During the Great Depression of the 1930s, the U.S. government had a program called the Civilian Conservation Corps, commonly known as the CCC, to provide work for young men from ages 18 to 25. They lived in camps like the one in Oronoco, learned skills, and in general were supervised as if they were in the army. The government sent a large portion of the young men's paychecks home to their families. As mentioned on another drive, the Blue Ridge Parkway was as a CCC project and the Parkway recently celebrated its 75th anniversary.
8.5 Turn right on Fiddler's Green Way (Rt.633).	Stay close to the right side of this road as Staton's Falls is in this area on the left. The falls may look innocent enough, but fatalities have occurred.
9.8 Fiddler's Green Way (Rt. 633) will soon end and join Coffeytown Road (Rt. 634).	The cabin in the large yard on the left is a site for picnics, reunions and, traditionally, a little bluegrass fiddling.
10.1 Stay left at this fork in the road.	

10.3

Continue on Coffey-
town Road (Rt. 634).

The Macedonia Church on the right, built in 1896, now serves as the main landmark for Alto (Coffeytown). Twice a year, in July and near Christmas, a homecoming is celebrated for everyone in or from the community. The building itself has just been named a national historic site. The interior was built of chestnut only a few years before the blight began destroying virtually all the chestnut trees in North America.

On the hill behind the church once stood the Coffeytown two-room school house. Teachers would board at the Coffey home/store, the two-story white building just next door.

11.7

Two options at this point:

Either turn around now for a slightly different return trip to Dodd's Ford

OR

Start Drive # 9 by going straight uphill as the state road becomes a National Forest road.

Those who are starting Drive #9 here might sometimes feel as if they are blazing their own mountain trail. The road is curvy and a bit rough for a few miles. It will eventually become a state road again, following Big Piney River down the mountain.

Turn to Drive #9 for more information.

11.8

For those who have chosen not to start Drive # 9 and who have just turned around, keep straight on Coffeytown Road (Rt. 634).

Some families still live in Coffeytown year-round and some have vacation homes here.

13.2

Just after the Macedonia Church, follow Coffeytown Road (Rt. 634) as it veers sharply to the left.

13.3

The old Coffey Cemetery is on the right.

14.6 **OPTIONAL** **DETOUR** For those who would like to take a long hike. At the conclusion of the hike, return to Coffeytown Rd.	On the left is Wiggins Spring Road (Rt. 755); this route leads to the national scenic area of Mt. Pleasant. A nicely marked hike leads to the top of Mt. Pleasant, the tallest mountain in Amherst County at over 4,000 feet. When seen from the traffic circle, the outline of the top of the mountain looks to some like a "sleeping giant," with Mt. Pleasant itself representing the giant's head.
17.3 Turn left on Amherst-Lexington Highway (Rt. 60).	Long Mt. Wayside is coming soon on the left. The wayside has picnic tables. The Appalachian Trail, which goes from Georgia to Maine, passes through here. In the past, Easter Sunrise Services were held here. To go on the optional detour mentioned below, first pull into the Long Mt. Wayside. Mt. Horeb Road begins there.
18.2 **OPTIONAL** **DETOUR**	Heading back east to the starting point, trip takers have a chance to take a short, steep, curvy, narrow, gravel detour on Mt. Horeb Road (Rt.686). Drivers will pass the Allen home where the six Allen brothers discussed in the book, *Civil War Letters*, lived before they went off to the Civil War; only four returned. They will also pass Mt. Horeb United Methodist Church, founded in 1844 and still active. They will turn left when Mt. Horeb Road (Rt. 686) returns to Amherst-Lexington Highway (Rt. 60). Amherst-Lexington Highway (Rt. 60) is full of little off-roads like this which were bypassed when old Rt. 13 was improved and renamed Rt. 60.
22.3 Dodd's Ford	Drive #8 ends here. To return to the Amherst Circle, keep going straight on the Amherst-Lexington Highway (Rt. 60) for approximately twelve miles.

9

Down from Coffeytown Along the Piney River Border

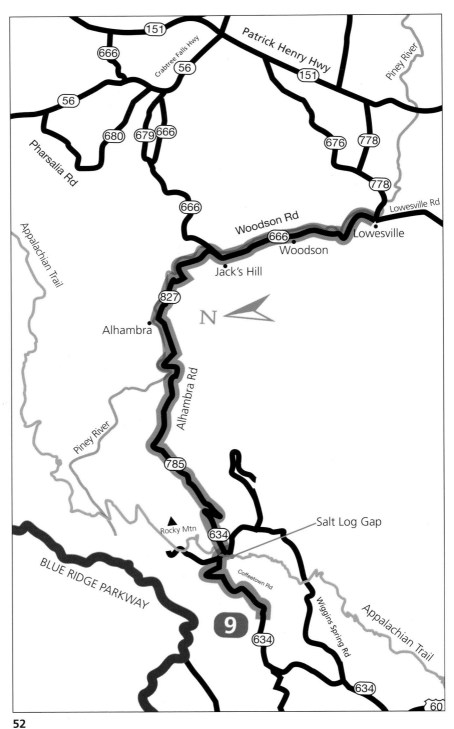

9

Down from Coffeytown Along the Piney River Border

PREVIEW:
Above the Blue Ridge Parkway is an area of mountain tops where Amherst, Nelson, and Rockbridge counties converge. Several rivers start as springs in this vicinity. It's a difficult area to find; as the old saying goes, "You can't get there from here; you have to go someplace else and start." This drive starts where Drive #8 ends—where the Forest Service takes over the road maintenance above Coffeytown on Rt. 634. From there, the road will basically follow Big Piney River down the mountain. Notice an intentional omission: very little commentary accompanies today's drive. Enjoy the lack of interruptions in the journey.

TOTAL MILES: 15.5

FROM THE AMHERST CIRCLE:

Go west on Rt. 60 about 16 miles. Turn right on Coffeytown Road (Rt. 634) and follow it as it veers right at the Coffey cemetery. Continue on Rt. 634 until reaching the sign for Forest Service maintenance.

MILES/DIRECTIONS	COMMENTARY
STARTING POINT Where Coffeytown Road (Rt. 634) ends and a sign tells drivers the Forest Service maintenance begins. About 1.5 miles from Macedonia Church.	Drive slowly on this steep, gravel, curvy, true "mountain road." The western edges of Amherst and Nelson counties actually fall within the boundaries of the only national forests in Virginia: George Washington and Thomas Jefferson. National forests are different from national parks in that they are allowed to have commercial uses. In mountainous areas, for instance, ski resorts might be built on national forest land. Commercial logging might take place. Only by special permission is part of a national forest declared a wilderness area, as is The Priest in Nelson County. A similar limitation, but not quite as restrictive, is the declaration of a scenic area, such as Mt. Pleasant in Amherst County.

MILES/DIRECTIONS	COMMENTARY
4.0	The road rises for a few miles until it passes Rocky Mountain (the one with towers on top), then begins to descend.
8.9 Just after Wiggins Spring Road enters from the right, what was Coffeytown Road (Rt. 634) has become Perkins Mill Road (Rt. 666).	Occasionally, a side road, such as Wiggins Spring Road, seems to appear out of nowhere. Save any such temptations for another time, and stay on the main road. In this general area is a place called Hog Camp Gap on the Appalachian Trail. Tradition notes that a hog camp was a place where mountain people turned out their hogs and let them forage. The usual season for this hog camp was the fall when nuts, especially chestnuts, fell off the trees. When the chestnut blight of the early 20th century wreaked havoc by killing virtually all the chestnut trees in America, especially in the eastern forests, many mountain people lost nice secondary incomes when there were no more chestnuts to collect and either sell or barter. The true economic impact, however, was in the loss of the valuable chestnut lumber.
12.0 Woodson Road (Rt. 666)	Piney River originates in these mountains and serves as the border between Amherst and Nelson Counties. During the long descent, the road eventually passes a few hunting cabins, then more permanent homes and churches.

13.3

Near here are the areas known as Alhambra and Woodson, both along the Piney River.

Woodson is named for David Woodson, a Civil War Marine who helped hold back Union soldiers on the James River near Richmond.

Another well-known member of the Woodson family was Dr. J.B. Woodson, a local doctor, state senator, and superintendent of the Piedmont Sanitarium.

In the 1930s, young men working for the New Deal CCC program lived in a camp nearby. In the 1940s, another group of young men camped just south of Woodson, this time they were soldiers in training to enter World War II. Later, they were known to have suffered heavy casualties in the invasion of Italy. One resident recalls that the American fliers had so few supplies to use for practicing bombing runs that they dropped bags of flour.

15.5

Drive #9 ends at the Rt. 666/Rt. 778 intersection at Lowesville.

TWO OPTIONS

Join Drive #10 by going left on Rt. 778.

OR

Turn right on Rt. 778. Go south until reaching the stop sign at Rt. 60. Turn left and drive about five miles east to return to the Amherst Circle.

10
Mansions, Railroads, and Minerals

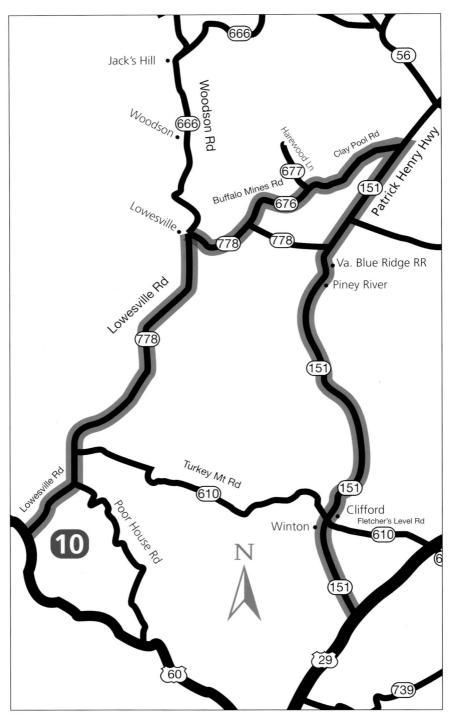

10

Mansions, Railroads, and Minerals

PREVIEW:
Drive #10 focuses on two eras of prosperity: 18th c. growth, visible now especially in a number of historic homes in the New Glasgow/Clifford area, and the 19th c. century addition of railroads. Locally, in the early 20th c., the study of a short-line railroad shows the reliance of the counties' economies on lumber and then on mining. The short-lived but significant mining industry of the mid-20th c. unearthed various minerals from a rich belt stretching for miles underground in parts of Amherst and Nelson Counties. When local scientists found new and lucrative uses for these minerals, hundreds of people in both counties benefited from employment opportunities.

TOTAL MILES: 20
FROM THE AMHERST CIRCLE:
Go 5.6 miles west on the Lexington Turnpike (Rt.60) until reaching the starting point at the corner of Lexington Turnpike (Rt. 60) and Lowesville Road (Rt. 778).

MILES/DIRECTIONS	COMMENTARY
STARTING POINT The corner of Lexington Turnpike (Rt.60) and Lowesville Road (Rt. 778)	Follow the Lowesville Road (Rt. 778) for almost seven miles.
1.2	Poor House Road is to the right. In past days of little government welfare, counties paid farmers to board the poor, but only if necessary. Such boarders were expected to work on the farm, if possible. One man living at the poorhouse was blind; he still chopped wood daily as his contribution.
1.4	Henley's Store, now unused and in disrepair, is on the right. Most maps call the neighborhood by the store's name.

59

2.3	At the corner of Sandidges Road (Rt. 632) is an old brick Masonic Temple. Formerly, this building belonged to Mt. Moriah Church, one of the oldest churches in Amherst County. When Mt. Moriah merged with Central Baptist in the middle of the 19th century, the trustees gave the building to the Masons.
4.4	Mt. View Market on the right is more than just a convenience store. It has a reputation for great food, especially sandwiches, and occasionally entertainment.
4.6	Temperance Elementary is similar to Pleasant View Elementary (Drive # 7) because it's a small school and serves the western part of the county.
5.7	The village of Lowesville lies ahead. Far back on the right is "Fairview," a bed-and-breakfast on the historic registry. According to its website (www.fairviewbedandbreakfast.com), it was built in the Italianate style just two years after the Civil War ended.
	Central Baptist Church, mentioned earlier, began with the merging of several smaller churches.
6.6	Several very old buildings remain here in the heart of Lowesville. The brick store on the right is another of Amherst County's historical landmarks. Built soon after the Civil War, the Hite store has served multiple functions for the community: a post office, the Lowesville Academy, and a boarding house. Compared to other country stores of the time, the Hite store is larger and more sophisticated in its architectural style.
6.8 Veer right, cross the bridge, and remain on Lowesville Road (Rt. 778).	The Piney River continues to serve as the border between Amherst and Nelson Counties. (Drive #9 comes down from Coffeytown and ends here.)

60

7.1

Lowesville can claim a second historic landmark, Woodson's Mill. Since the mill is across the river from Hite's store, however, this time the landmark lies in Nelson County. Even though Woodson's Mill was built over two centuries ago, it has been restored to good running condition, thus conserving both the building and the process. Someone observing this milling process might realize that the "modern" trend toward local organic food is really very traditional. (www.woodsonsmill.com)

7.7
Turn left on Buffalo Mines Road (Rt. 676).

Note the name of the road. In the early 20th century, several mining businesses extracted various minerals from the ground. Two nearby plants were Carolina Minerals and Dominion Minerals, which processed a fine green rock, aplite, mainly used to polish glass. Although most mineral plants have closed, some rock pits and several active stone operations remain as do names such as Buffalo Mines Road and Quarry Road.

Today, observers driving down Buffalo Mines Road would see little evidence of mining operations. Instead, they would see evidence of one of Nelson County's strongest economic assets—the orchard industry. Depending on the season, they might see peach trees in bloom or apple trees laden with fruit. These particular fruit trees are part of Saunders Brothers Orchard.

9.4

Nearby is "Harewood," a Cabell house thought by some to be named after "Harewood House" in England. Much more accepted, however, is the assumption that, because Dr. William Hare lived in it with his children and mother-in-law in the early 18th century, the house was named for him. Mrs. Hare had died young, so her mother, the recently widowed Hannah Carrington Cabell, moved to "Harewood" to help rear her grandchildren. A Harewood School was once here and the Harewood Cemetery is slightly beyond the house.

MILES/DIRECTIONS	COMMENTARY
10.1 At the St. James Church intersection, continue straight on Rt. 676. The route stays the same, but the road name changes from Buffalo Mines to Clay Pool.	St. James Baptist Church has an active congregation. In addition to their regular services, members celebrate homecomings with out-of-town speakers and special music. Many country churches do the same.
12.0. After the stop sign, take a sharp right onto Patrick Henry Highway (Rt. 151).	
14.0 **OPTIONAL** **STOP**	On the left is the former headquarters of the Virginia Blue Ridge Railroad. Starting in the early-20th c., this small steam-powered railroad (eventually diesel-powered), with only twelve miles of track, carried the fast-disappearing chestnut logs out of the mountains to the Southern Railroad depot. It carried other products, also. In the 1930s, discoveries of four minerals were made in the area. These were to become very useful in business. After several decades of scrambling to prosper when the logging ended, the railroad joined the counties in reaping the benefits of the newly lucrative mining industry. Since the closing of the railroad, a recreational use has been found for this property, plus a right-of-way given by neighbors. A hiking, biking, and walking trail is now available to the public. Stop and enjoy.

14.3

Almost immediately following the railroad office is the unused Piney River Plant.

In its heyday, starting in the early 1940s, the plant employed hundreds of workers, including many scientists, engineers, and executives. The main output from the plant was titanium dioxide, a product used in paint. When environmental problems arose during an expanded national focus on cleaner air and water, the company opted to move some of the work and employees elsewhere. The plant closed in the early 1970s after four decades of providing many good jobs for the people of Amherst and Nelson counties.

14.6

Here is the Piney River bridge, part of the border between Nelson and Amherst counties.

For the next 5 miles until the end of Drive #10

In this vicinity of the New Glasgow/Clifford Historic District are several significant 18th c. and early-19th c. buildings. As in other areas filled with important old houses, such as Drive #4, directions remain less specific than they would be for a house tour. All five of the houses mentioned below are or were on the national historic landmarks list.

Two of the houses have roads named for them. "Athlone," an early-18th c. frame house, burned in 1996, but has been completely reconstructed. The state removed it from the landmark list after the fire. Also honored by a road named for it is "Geddes," a mid-18th c. frame house. It belonged to Rev. Robert Rose, then to his son Hugh Rose, the husband of one of the prominent Cabells. During the American Revolution, the Roses provided a safe haven for Gov. Thomas Jefferson and his family when British soldiers were hoping to capture them at "Monticello."

On Fletcher's Level (Rt. 610) near Patrick Henry Highway (Rt. 151) is "The Brick House," built by "King David" Garland circa 1800; on Patrick Henry Highway (Rt. 151) near North Amherst Highway (Rt. 29) is the often-remodeled "Glebe," built for St. Mark's Church soon after Amherst became a county.

No longer a private home and no longer in the Clifford area, "Tusculum" was built in 1735 by the grandfather of Sweet Briar College's founder. Almost three centuries later, because it was showing signs of disrepair and blocking development, "Tusculum" was donated to Sweet Briar with the goal of rebuilding it. Movers carefully dismantled the house and stored it in numbered pieces on the SBC campus, where it is today.

19.4–19.6 OPTIONAL STOPS

In the center of Clifford and fairly close together are three historic sites well worth the time to visit.

First is St. Mark's Church, a brick structure built circa 1815. It still has an active congregation. On the grounds is an old cemetery.

Next is "Winton," a frame house built in the late-18th century by Col. Joseph Cabell. The house is now part of a country club and is on the national landmarks list.

Just past the driveway to Winton is a sign directing visitors to a cemetery which is open to the public. Patrick Henry's mother is buried there. In her later years, she lived at Winton with her daughter and family, the Merediths. The story goes that Sarah Henry's son-in-law admired her so much that he asked to be buried at her feet, in hopes that he would see her first on Judgment Day.

20.0

The corner of Patrick Henry Highway (Rt. 151) and North Amherst Highway (Rt. 29) marks the end of Drive #10.

To return to the Amherst Circle, turn right and drive 3.5 miles.

11

Tobacco Row Mountain and the Orchards

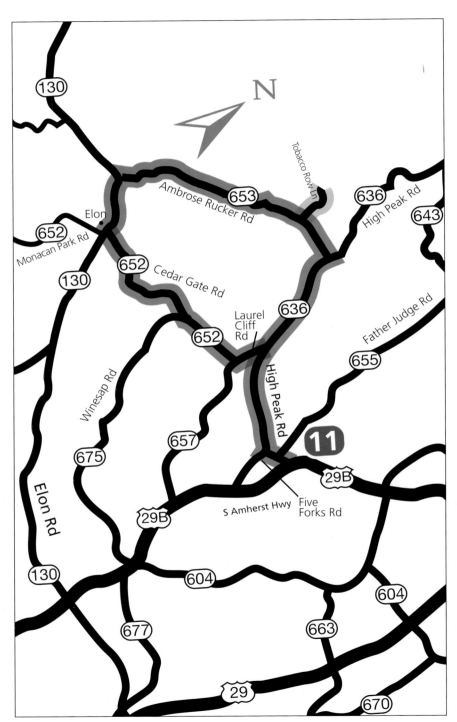

11

Tobacco Row Mountain and the Orchards

PREVIEW:

At just under 3,000 feet, Tobacco Row Mountain is not the tallest mountain in Amherst County, but certainly one of the most noticeable. As its name indicates, tobacco was once a main cash crop. As tobacco yield dwindled, local farmers began to plant apple orchards on and near Tobacco Row Mountain. In recent years, almost all of those orchards have gone out of business. Nelson County, on the other hand, still has at least six active orchards. Today's drive on Ambrose Rucker Road will reveal buildings or signs from many of the old orchards and permit a stop at a working orchard.

TOTAL MILES: 13.0

FROM THE AMHERST CIRCLE:

Go south on Amherst Highway (Rt. 29 Business) until just past Faulconerville at the corner of Five Forks (Rt. 671).

MILES/DIRECTIONS	COMMENTARY
STARTING POINT	Go southwest on Five Forks Road (Rt. 671), passing Father Judge Road (Rt. 655) on the right.
At the corner of Amherst Highway (Rt. 29 Business) and Five Forks Road (Rt. 671).	The name for Father Judge Road came from a former 1960s Catholic Seminary. Currently the building is a Job Corps site.

MILES/DIRECTIONS	COMMENTARY
0.4 Turn right on High Peak Road (Rt. 636)	Straight ahead is a sweeping view of Tobacco Row Mountain, which stretches about 10 miles from Elon Road (Rt. 130) to Amherst-Lexington Highway (Rt. 60). High Peak Road, aptly named for its view, actually crosses the mountain. If this drive kept going on High Peak Road (Rt. 636), it would go through Ware's Gap on Ware's Gap Road (still Rt. 636) and to Puppy Creek Road near Pleasant View. Another possibility for High Peak Road to cross Tobacco Row Mountain would be to turn off Rt. 636 onto Wagon Trail Road (Rt. 643), now a totally paved road, and end up in Pedlar Mills. Both Pleasant View and Pedlar Mills are part of Drive #7.
2.0 Immediately past the church is the next turn.	On the right is Bethany United Methodist Church, founded in the late-19th century. Bethany Church was among the last to have a lawn party, a holdover from a not-so-distant past when practically every country church hosted a summer gathering where all could enjoy home-fried chicken, freshly-picked garden vegetables, and homemade ice cream. The women of the church now have a fall bazaar instead of the lawn party.
2.1 Turn left on Laurel Cliff Road (Rt. 657)	The road is named for "Laurel Cliff," a late-19th c. large brick house on the right. Two huge barns remain from the farm's days as a dairy.
2.6 Turn right on Cedar Gate Road (Rt. 652)	For several miles the road passes a residential area which gradually becomes more populated in approaching the village of Elon.
5.3	On the right is Elon Presbyterian Church. The church, established in the early-19th century, has continued to thrive, as has its nearby church neighbor, Elon Baptist Church.
5.4 Turn right on Elon Road (Rt. 130) Immediately past the mansion is the next turn.	The large rock house on the hill on the right has been called by a number of names; among them are "Stonehurst" (the name currently outside the home), "Rock Castle," "Dillard Mansion," and "The Shelter" (the name the Dillards gave it). It is said that David Hugh Dillard instructed his architect to make the house both water- and fire-proof.

Dillard had earlier renovated "The Wigwam" where folk artist Queena Stovall (as previously mentioned in Drive #2) lived with her family. Queena Stovall was one of David Hugh Dillard's eleven brothers and sisters.

6.3

Turn right on Ambrose Rucker Road (Rt. 653). Go slowly and stay to the right on this narrow and curvy mountain road.

This road is named for Ambrose Rucker, a wealthy landowner and Revolutionary War patriot who also founded one of the earliest Episcopal churches in the area. Two of his brothers, Anthony and Benjamin, invented the batteau.

A batteau is a long, narrow cargo boat made especially to carry hogsheads of tobacco down the James River. The boat is easily maneuvered for two reasons. First, it has neither bow nor stern, but looks the same at both ends, like a fifty-foot canoe. Second, it rides higher than most boats even when filled with almost a dozen thousand-pound barrels; therefore, it does not often get hung up on rocks in shallow water.

At the end of his life, Thomas Jefferson had one more connection with Amherst County. It happened when a patent dispute arose in the 1820s. Jefferson agreed to speak for the Rucker brothers' heirs and to verify he had seen the batteau when the Ruckers first made it. The dispute disappeared. Every June, Lynchburg and other stops along the James host a Batteau Festival.

Perhaps because of a belief that peaches and apples grow best on the protected side of a mountain, this road once connected many working orchards. Although most of those orchards are out of business now, many of their buildings can still be seen along the road. Some include, in order, Speed-the-Plough (currently a bed-and-breakfast on the national landmark list), Montrose, Shepherd, and Rucker Orchards. Last on the road, Morris Orchard is still thriving under the ownership of a younger generation of the same family. Because of the large number of apple orchards in Amherst County at one time, the Elon Home Demonstration Club started a small apple harvest festival in the early 1970s.

Today, at apple harvest time, Amherst County High School is the site of a widely expanded fall festival.

9.4
OPTIONAL
DETOUR
Turn left on Tobacco Row Lane, then take the right fork of the driveway to the packing shed.

Upon finishing the visit, return to the entrance of Morris Orchard and turn left on Ambrose Rucker Road (Rt. 653).

Morris Orchard is open from mid-June to Christmas and, depending on the season, has for sale apples, peaches, blackberries, blueberries, pumpkins, and Christmas trees. Apples and apple cider are the specialty, however.

9.9
Turn right on High Peak Road (Rt. 636)

An interest of many people these days is local food, whether they raise a garden, own one fruit tree, buy directly from a farmer, stop at a vegetable stand, participate in a co-op, or . . . .

An offshoot of the local food movement is the search for wider varieties of certain foods, like apples. Near here was the nursery/orchard of a well-known heirloom apple expert, Thomas Burford, and his late brother Russell. Read one of his books or be alert for a chance to hear him speak about perpetuating old varieties of apples.

13.0
Turn left on Five Forks (Rt. 671)

The end of the trip is at the corner of Five Forks Road (Rt. 671) and Amherst Highway (Rt. 29 Business).

To return to the Amherst Circle, turn left on Amherst Highway (Rt. 29 Business). Go about 8 miles north.

12

Meandering Across Amherst County on Route 610

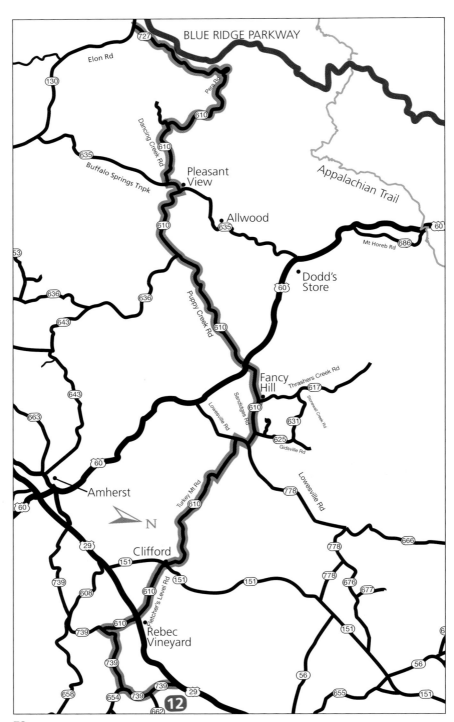

BLUE RIDGE PARKWAY

Elon Rd

130

Pera Rd

610

Dancing Creek Rd

610

635

Buffalo Springs Tnpk

Pleasant
View

Allwood

635

Appalachian Trail

60

Mt Horeb Rd

686

53

636

636

643

Puppy Creek Rd

610

Dodd's
Store

60

Fancy
Hill

Thrashers Creek Rd

617

643

Lowesville Rd

Sandidges Rd

610

Stonewall Creek Rd

663

631

625

Gidsville Rd

60

Lowesville Rd

778

Amherst

Turkey Mt Rd

610

N

60

666

29

Clifford

778

151

778

739

151

151

676

608

610

Fletcher's Level Rd

151

677

739

610

Rebec
Vineyard

151

6

739

56

739

56

658

654

739

739

29

655

151

12

662

12

Meandering Across Amherst County on Route 610

PREVIEW:

Amherst and Nelson counties currently have just one primary four-lane divided highway: Route 29, which runs north and south. Other well-known roads, for instance, Route 60 and Route 130, do the same for direct travel east and west. These main roads substitute for Amherst and Nelson's nonexistent interstates and carry most of the commercial traffic. Most of the counties' roads are, of course, not through roads. Once in a while, however, a back road like Route 610 will end up crossing an entire county, and in a sense becoming a through road. This drive follows Route 610—one of the county's longest roads—as it meanders across Amherst County.

TOTAL MILES: 31
FROM THE AMHERST CIRCLE:

Follow North Amherst Highway (Rt. 29) 8.1 miles to Tye River Road (Rt. 739). Be on alert for a one-lane underpass at 9.1 miles. Today's drive begins a total of 10.1 miles from the circle when the road's name changes to Boxwood Farm Road.

MILES/DIRECTIONS	COMMENTARY
STARTING POINT Boxwood Farm Road (Rt. 739)	There is some discrepancy among maps as to exactly where Rt. 610 begins and ends.
1.8 Rt. 610 splits off to the right under the name of New Glasgow Road. Follow Rt. 610 for the entire drive. Even though the route number remains the same, the road name will change seven times.	Maps call this area east of Rt. 29 New Glasgow. The community of Clifford is on the west side of Rt. 29. What can be confusing, however, is that the former name for Clifford was New Glasgow.

MILES/DIRECTIONS	COMMENTARY
2.4	St. Paul's Baptist Church sits back on the right. Notice the unusual roof line.
3.8 **OPTIONAL DETOUR** At the stop sign, turn right onto Rt. 29 north. Get into the left lane to make the first u-turn possible onto Rt. 29 south. Turn right into Rebec Vineyards. When ready to leave Rebec Vineyard, continue south on Rt. 29 and take the first right on Fletcher's Level (Rt. 610).	The Rebec Vineyards are open almost every day and are home to a wine and garlic festival the second weekend each October. The private home on the property, "Mountainview," was originally built on top of Spencer's Mountain in the early 18th c. It was then called "Spencer's Plantation." In the late 18th c. the owner, Dr. Paul Cabell, moved the house to its present location. The house is listed as a state and national historic landmark.
3.8 **FOR THOSE SKIPPING THE OPTIONAL DETOUR...** After the stop sign, stay on Rt. 610 to cross Rt. 29 carefully, as it is a four-lane divided highway.	
4.0 Rt. 610 is now called Fletcher's Level Road.	The Fletcher name comes from Amherst County and Sweet Briar College history. The founder of SBC was Indiana Fletcher Williams. Her father, Elijah Fletcher, had come to Amherst County from Vermont as a tutor to the Crawford children and others at the New Glasgow Academy. He later married one of his students, Maria Crawford. "Tusculum," their home, is a national historic landmark, currently dismantled and stored at SBC. When it was the Crawford-Fletcher family home, it was near here. The community of Clifford, formerly known as New Glasgow, is located on Patrick Henry Highway (Rt. 151), the road Rt. 610 is about

to cross. The area of New Glasgow/Clifford has been listed as a national historic district. Many of the important buildings are still standing.

5.1

At the stop sign turn right on Patrick Henry Highway (Rt. 151/610). Almost immediately turn left on Rt. 610, now called Turkey Mountain Road.

Part of Turkey Mountain Road is gravel.

9.7
OPTIONAL
DETOUR
Follow signs to Mill Creek Lake, if desired.

Route 610 passes all three of Amherst County's flood control/recreational lakes. Each lake allows boating and fishing, but no motor boating and no swimming.

10.7
Turn right at the stop sign onto Lowesville Road (Rt. 778/610).

11.0
Very shortly, turn left on Sandidges Road (Rt. 610)

The Masonic Temple on the left is discussed on Drive #10. Notice the gorgeous view.

11.5
OPTIONAL
DETOUR
Follow signs to Stone House Lake, if desired.

12.5
OPTIONAL
DETOUR
Follow signs to Thrasher's Lake, if desired. Notice that Sandidges Road (Rt. 610) goes left here.

The white house on the left at this intersection is called "Fancy Hill." The original house was built in the early 1800s by the Bowles family. It was still in that family in the 1950s when it burned and was rebuilt in the Williamsburg style. The current owners have added to the house.

13.2
Notice several old buildings on the right and left.

13.7	Emmanuel Baptist Church, on the right, was organized in the early 20th century with about sixty members and has been active ever since that time. This 1907 building is in a modified gothic style.
13.9 After the stop sign, cross Route 60 and continue to follow Route 610. For the next seven miles the name of the road is Puppy Creek Road.	On this road are various landmarks: the old Massie home, which is known as "Boulder Springs" or "Edgewood" and is on the national landmark list; the old Eubank home, "Walnut Hill"; Kersey Road, which goes to Allwood; and Ware's Gap Road, which crosses Tobacco Row Mountain.
21.1 At the stop sign in Pleasant View, turn left onto Buffalo Springs Turnpike (Rt. 635/610).	New Prospect Baptist Church met here in the early-19th century with beginnings at Maple Creek Meeting House about fifty years earlier. Drive #7 goes into more detail about the founding of the church.
21.8 Turn right on Dancing Creek Road (Rt. 610).	Pleasant View Elementary School is one of the smallest schools in the county with one class per grade. It serves a wider but less-populated area than do all the other elementary schools except Temperance. One principal serves both schools.
24.1 Veer right as Rt. 610 becomes Pera Road.	Very soon on the left is a modern memorial for Little Ottie Powell, a youngster who wandered off in 1891 and was found several months later, having died from exposure. Another marker was placed where young Powell's body was found. This marker is several miles away but far from any road.
30.6 After a sharp horseshoe curve, Route 610 ends at the intersection with Cheatham Road. Continue driving straight until a stop sign at the intersection of Elon Road (Rt. 130).	Today's drive has ended. Route 610 stops just a few miles short of the James River, thus not quite traversing the entire county. To return to the Amherst traffic circle, turn left on Elon Road (Rt. 130), go about 15 miles to Rt. 29 Business. Turn left and go about 10 miles.

13

View from Bear Mountain

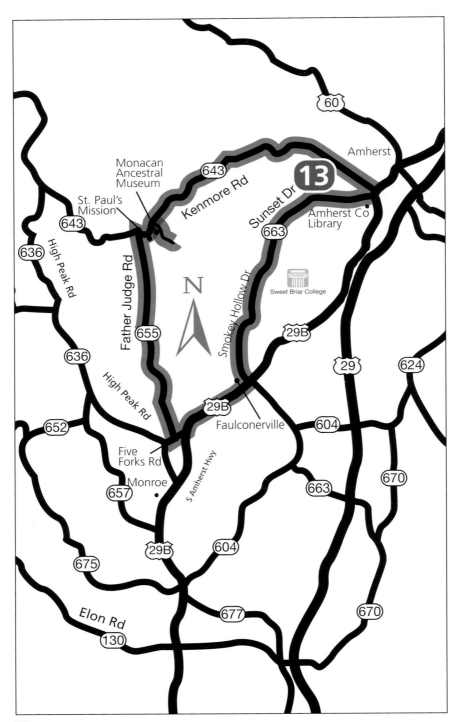

13

View from Bear Mountain

PREVIEW:

The focus of today's drive is the Monacan Indian Tribe. The tribe's Amherst County homeland, in the area from Bethel on the James River to Bear Mountain, has only gradually and with great effort become legally owned by the tribe. Help came from, among others, the Episcopal Church, especially the Rev. Arthur Grey, who set up a mission and a school for the Monacans. At different times, depending on the mood of the legislatures, national and state laws either conflicted with or promoted the Monacan goals. Currently, in 2012, Monacans have been pleased to hear that U.S. Senator James Webb called for federal recognition of all Native American tribes in Virginia.

Be prepared to see the typical Amherst County scenes of beautiful mountains and historic homes both before and after visiting an even earlier historic "home," Bear Mountain.

TOTAL MILES: ABOUT 15
FROM THE AMHERST CIRCLE:

Drive south for 2 miles on Rt. 29 Business. Turn right on Kenmore Road (Rt. 643). Immediately, turn left onto Sunset Drive (Rt. 663).

MILES/DIRECTIONS	COMMENTARY
STARTING POINT Behind the Amherst Library at the beginning of Sunset Drive (Rt. 663).	Once known as Old Bethel Road, Sunset Drive is a suburban road whose modern homes are interspersed with a few historic houses. Among the 18th and 19th c. homes are "Edge Hill," "Retreat Plantation," "White Hall," and "Locust Grove." A generation of youngsters from the Amherst area no doubt remembers the Fourth of July fireworks extravaganza put on each year by the Pixley family at "Locust Grove."
2.0 The name of Rt. 663 changes from Sunset Drive to Smokey Hollow.	

MILES/DIRECTIONS	COMMENTARY
4.0	Rt. 663 goes behind Sweet Briar College, a nationally-recognized women's college. The main entrance to the college is on Rt. 29. The entire campus is on the national landmark list as Sweet Briar College Historic District in 1995; "Sweet Briar House" was listed separately 25 years earlier. Tours of the campus are available, see www.sbc.edu
4.9 Turn right on Rt. 29 Business after the stop sign. Go south for about 3 miles.	This community of Faulconerville is named after the Faulconer family whose old family home is slightly behind the stores.
6.1 Turn right on Five Forks Road (Rt. 671).	This intersection is where Drive #11 began, so the area will be somewhat familiar.
6.4 Right on Father Judge Road (Rt. 655).	
8.9 Job Corps Center	As mentioned before, this road got its name from a 1960s Catholic Seminary, which is currently a Job Corps center. The large campus boards out-of-town young people while they learn skills to get and keep a job.
10.1 Turn right at Crawford's Store onto Kenmore Road (Rt. 643).	

**13.5
OPTIONAL
STOP**
Turn right onto
Indian Mission Road
(Rt. 780).

On this home site of the Monacan Indian
Nation are several buildings. Among them is
the national historic landmark named "Bear
Mountain Indian Mission School."

Visitors who wish to go inside the mission,
church, and school should check the website:
www.monacannation.com/museum. Groups are
welcomed and tours can be arranged.

When leaving, turn
right onto Kenmore
Road (Rt. 643).

Interestingly enough, although some road and
business names in Amherst and Nelson Counties
refer to the Seminole Indian Tribe, more recent
scholarship indicates that while other tribes may
have preceded the Monacans, the Seminoles
were not among them. Cherokees, however,
may have been here. Naming in honor of the
Monacans has begun with, for instance, the
James River bridge on the new Rt. 29 is officially
the Monacan Bridge.

Another point is that the years of segregation
affected the Native Americans as well as blacks
and whites.

Because Amherst schools had only two
segregated groups and required African-
Americans and Native Americans to go to school
together, most Monacans chose to segregate
themselves for schooling at the St. Paul's mission.

As the 20th century began, a founder of a
private school in Virginia would have to specify
both the race and sex of the students at the
proposed school. Sweet Briar College, for
example, was founded in 1901 by Indiana
Fletcher Williams as a memorial for her late
daughter, Daisy. Mrs. Williams specified that the
school was for "white girls and young women."
Sixty years later, when Sweet Briar trustees
were trying to integrate the college, they were
finally able to do so because Mrs. Williams'
specification was required by the law at that
time—a law that would not have been allowed
in the 1960s.

Later, when total integration of public schools came along, it affected all students, whether Indian, black, or white. As in the present day, all children began going to school together, no matter what race or sex they were.

At least two books have recently been written about Indian tribes in the Amherst area. One by Horace Rice, *The Buffalo Ridge Cherokee: A Remnant of a Great Nation Divided,* expressed Rice's theories about Cherokees in Central Virginia.

The beginnings of another book came when Dr. Peter Houck, a Lynchburg pediatrician, noticed Indian characteristics in some of his patients. Once he found out a few things about the Monacan Indians, he became fascinated with the tribe. The result of his research is a book which he entitled *Indian Island in Amherst County.*

14.7
Follow Kenmore Road about 4 miles back to Rt. 29 Business, where the drive ends.

Kenmore Road is named for an old estate, "Kenmore," built by Samuel Garland. In the late-19th c., Henry A. Strode married Judge Garland's grand-daughter. Strode later bought Kenmore and used the main house as a preparatory school for the University of Virginia. According to a newspaper advertisement in 1882, a boarding student would pay $300 for the year. He would study, among other subjects, Greek and Latin, as well as mathematics from algebra through calculus. Running Kenmore School must have prepared Henry Strode also, as he later became president of Clemson University.

To return to the circle, turn left on Rt. 29 Business and head north for about 2 miles.

14

Hurricane Camille, Part 1: The Massies Mill Area

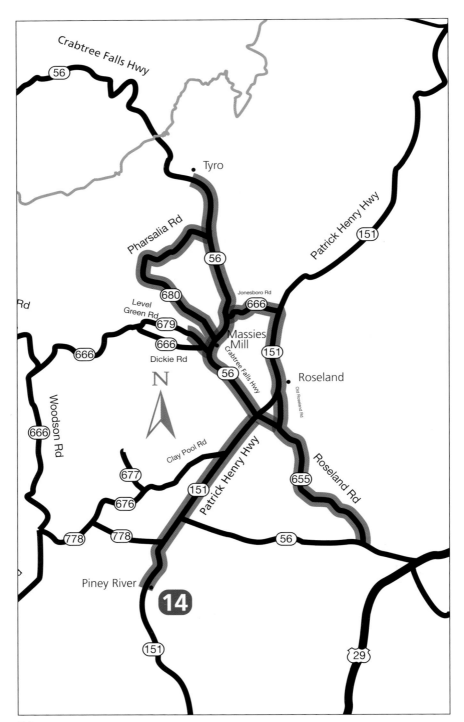

14

Hurricane Camille, Part 1: The Massies Mill Area

PREVIEW

This drive will encompass one of the focal points in the first phases of Hurricane Camille's destruction the night of August 19-20, 1969. The remnant of the hurricane, after significant damage and loss of life along the Gulf Coast two days earlier, reorganized as it converged with a weather system swinging eastward from the Midwest, and inflicted its wrath upon the eastern slope of the Blue Ridge Mountains.

An already wet summer had saturated the ground, and the addition of what is believed to be one of the largest rainfalls ever registered, as much as 30 inches of rain in a 5-hour period, caused an avalanche of water, mud, trees, and boulders, and wreaked havoc upon everything in its path.

This trip will be much more meaningful when accompanied by familiarity with pictures, maps, and personal accounts from any of these sources: *Torn Land* (Simpson, 1970), *Nelson County Virginia Heritage 1807-2000* (2001), *Roar of the Heavens* (Bechtel, 2006), *Heartbeats of Nelson* (Saunders, 2007).

TOTAL MILES: 22

FROM THE AMHERST CIRCLE:

Take Rt. 29-N 3.9 miles to Rt. 151-N, left onto Patrick Henry Highway. Proceed 6.2 miles to the border of Nelson County, delineated by the Piney River.

MILES/DIRECTIONS	COMMENTARY
STARTING POINT Crossing point of Rt. 151 and Piney River	A Virginia Historical Marker, located 0.1 mi. before the bridge, gives a brief history of Nelson County and its origin. There is not a good place here to stop the car.
	Hurricane Camille sent the Piney River out of its banks, filling the low-lying areas. Residents of houses on the left escaped the rising river by climbing to the second story or roof.

MILES/DIRECTIONS	COMMENTARY
Nelson County line	This bridge, as well as more than 100 others, had to be replaced after the August 1969 events; either the bridges were washed away, or the rushing water destroyed the approaches and left wide chasms between road and bridge.
0.2	Water rose to window level at American Cyanamid (on right), a thriving chemical industrial plant, Nelson County's largest employer at the time. Many stunned workers were trapped in the main office building as they witnessed their cars washing away from the parking lot. Communication with the outside became virtually impossible as phone and electric lines were damaged throughout the area. Workers at Cyanamid used hand signals to the Piney River Fire Department members who were across the flooded valley.
4.2 Turn left onto Crabtree Falls Highway, Rt. 56-W.	The Tye River runs parallel on the right. High into the trees lining the banks of the river, an assortment of debris—uprooted vegetation, parts of buildings, cars, or farm equipment, home furnishings, clothing—was visible long after 1969. The house on the knoll (left) was barely above water, seemingly on an island. The swollen Tye River filled the bottomland and became a torrent that raged unimpeded to the next lowest point, damaging everything in its path. Many who were directly involved in the rescue and recovery effort spoke of the tremendous stench that poured from the upturned virgin soil, and from the bodies of cattle, wildlife, and even birds that were killed by the surge of water.
6.0 Tye River Memorial Park	Crabtree Falls Highway, relatively straight at this point, crosses the Tye River a number of times as it flows its serpentine course from high in the mountains. The high point along the road lies near Fleetwood School. Several motorists spent the night marooned in their cars, but above the waterline. The small Tye River Memorial Park, in memory of the victims of Hurricane Camille, was dedicated in 1995.

6.1
Massies Mill

Massies Mill, formerly a village that thrived as a product of the timber industry prior to 1920, had a railroad spur and once-a-day passenger service to the Southern RR depot at Tye River. The town, which also featured residences, a bank, churches, stores, and businesses, some of which supported the nearby farming and orchard industry, now shows little evidence of commerce.

The devastation left by Hurricane Camille dramatically altered the way people lived and accelerated the abandonment of the town. One publication painted Massies Mill as a town that was both "put onto the map" and "removed from the map" by Hurricane Camille.

Grace Episcopal Church (right), founded in 1889, suffered extensive damage, but remained standing, with its back wall having been slammed against the altar. Restoration of the church was done by a group from the Mennonite disaster relief effort, as well as by members of the congregation and other angels of relief.

The work of the Mennonites cannot be overstated. They came from the Shenandoah Valley and other areas and worked diligently for more than a year, assisting in search and rescue, clean-up, and construction. With their own crops maturing in the fields at home, one stated, "Those at home can take care of the harvest. We need to be here."

Their humble and selfless work was so exemplary of the principle of helping people in need that a Baptist minister in Nelson County went on to found a similar program with the state Southern Baptist organization.

On the one-year anniversary of Hurricane Camille, new stained glass windows were dedicated at Grace Episcopal. These windows depicted both Noah and the Ark and the Hurricane Camille flood.

6.2

Just off Crabtree Falls Highway, to the right, stood the Massies Mill Presbyterian Church, built in 1898, and its nearby manse. The church was destroyed by the onslaught of water and debris; the manse remains.

MILES/DIRECTIONS	COMMENTARY
6.5 Rt. 56-W	A new Massies Mill Presbyterian Church was built, with help from the congregation and the Blue Ridge Presbytery.
Continue west on Route 56.	Rt. 56-W passes through pasture and cropland between Massies Mill and Tyro. This Tye River bottomland has been farmed for multiple generations. Today's scene belies the horrors of the night of August 19–20, 1969.
	Early in the spring when the river is fairly high, kayakers and canoeists are drawn to the Tye.
	The village of Tyro is quiet, as well. The Tye River in this area has always featured many "river jacks," the typical rocks worn smooth by centuries of water flowing over them. These rocks can be seen used in construction of houses, foundations, cabins, and walls. Additional rocks and boulders from the mountains were brought by the rushing waters. Sometimes the onrush of boulders and debris caused destruction; other times it created a protective barrier and saved lives and property.
9.8 Turn around and go east on Rt. 56.	Silver Creek–Seaman Apples, Inc., on the left, provides a good turn-around spot. Here the flood waters entered the packing shed and delayed the apple packing season until the mud and debris could be cleared.
11.1 Right turn onto Pharsalia Rd., Rt. 680	Rt. 680 will lead through orchards, vineyards, and pastures where cattle graze in picturesque surroundings.
12.8	The main house at Pharsalia was built in 1814. It now is used as the site of meetings, small conferences, and special events such as wedding receptions.
	After the storm, travel to the outside by road was virtually impossible, necessitating the dispatching of a helicopter to transport an expectant mother from near here. The newborn was delivered at Virginia Baptist Hospital soon thereafter.
	Helicopters provided the most reliable means for access to areas where people were trapped or missing, as well as for delivery of food, water, and other supplies.

15.2
Turn right onto Rt. 56-E.

Pharsalia Road loops around to reconnect with Rt. 56, Crabtree Falls Highway.

15.3
Turn right onto Dickie Road, Rt. 666.

This is the site of the old mill, the source of the name of the town.

15.6
Turn right onto Level Green Road, Rt. 679

15.9

Oak Hill Baptist Church

(Note: There are two Oak Hill Baptist Churches in Nelson County, both have nearby cemeteries, and both lost members to Hurricane Camille. The other is in the Davis Creek area.)

The history of Oak Hill Baptist Church is tied to that of Jonesboro Baptist Church. Oak Hill was established in 1869. It is documented that Jonesboro's original congregation included up to 250 Negroes who had attended services there. These congregants formed their own church and named it Oak Hill because of its setting.

Several victims of Hurricane Camille are buried in the church cemetery.

Turn around in the church parking lot and make the left turn to retrace the route via Level Green Road back to Dickie Road.

16.3
Turn left onto Dickie Road.

16.6
Turn left to drive through Massies Mill, Rt. 56-W, Crabtree Falls Highway.

Dickie Road intersects with Rt. 56-W, Crabtree Falls Highway.

Pass through Massies Mill again.

17.2
Turn right onto Jonesboro Road, Rt. 666.

18.6
Rt. 666, Jonesboro Road intersects with Rt. 151-S.

Jonesboro Church's origins date to 1806 and served a variety of denominations in the early years. Jonesboro is now affiliated with the Southern Baptist Convention. More than a dozen victims of Hurricane Camille are buried in the cemetery.

MILES/DIRECTIONS	COMMENTARY
20.3 Right turn onto Patrick Henry Highway, Rt. 151-S, to Rt. 723, Old Roseland Road, on left.	It was in this area that Sheriff Bill Whitehead lived. He awakened to unaccustomed noises: the roar of the creek, the downpour of rain, the crash of mudslides. Upon surveying the region by car, Sheriff Whitehead quickly faced the same difficulties as all other rescue and relief personnel. His first awareness of human loss was provided by a nearby resident whose family members had been swept away by the rising flood waters. Inaccessibility and remoteness of the affected areas combined to make the horrors wrought by Hurricane Camille very much an unknown phenomenon from the outset. Police and sheriff's department radios provided the only means of communication with the outside world. Residents and officials worked diligently and creatively to assess the situation as rapidly as possible, finding high water filling the valleys and facing other obstacles seemingly at every turn. They were forced to improvise or use any means available, first to rescue, then to sustain and recover. The tally of known fatalities was, after many weeks, finally assessed at about 125.
21.2 Turn left onto Old Roseland Road to Roseland Road (Rt. 655).	Hat Creek on left runs parallel to Old Roseland Road and empties into the Tye River at that point. The Roseland Post Office and several other buildings stood in this area, known as Old Roseland. The post office was uprooted and crashed to a site nearby. Two other businesses were destroyed.

This concludes Part 1 of the Hurricane Camille tour.

Part 2 of the Hurricane Camille tour starts in Lovingston, a left onto Rt. 29 North.

Rt. 29 can be reached by a left turn onto Roseland Road, Rt. 655. Proceed 3.4 mi., then another left turn onto Rt. 56, Tye Brook Highway, (1.1 mi.).

Another option is to return to Rt. 151, a right turn onto Roseland Road, 0.5 mi.

15

Hurricane Camille Tour, Part 2: Lovingston and Davis Creek

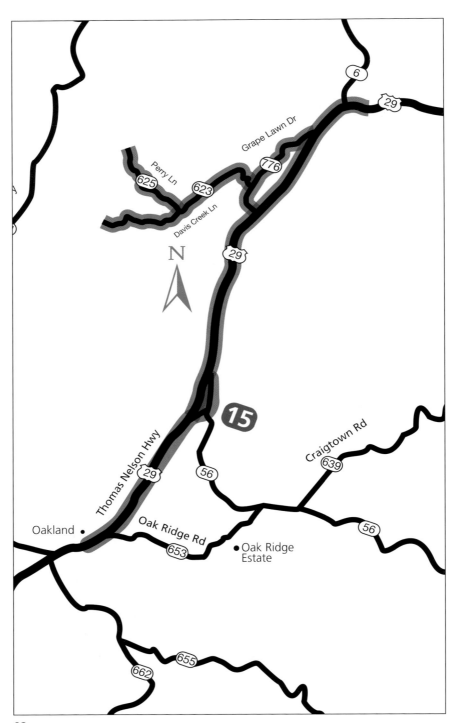

15

Hurricane Camille Tour, Part 2: Lovingston and Davis Creek

PREVIEW

This drive, through another part of Nelson County that was ravaged by the torrential rains of Hurricane Camille, will reveal the route of one woman's almost unbelievable journey in the water on the night of August 19-20, 1969. Also included are views of the narrow hollows where extended families lived – and perished – as water, mud, trees, and boulders plunged down the mountainside.

More than four decades of recovery and growth of vegetation have obscured much of the physical damage. The streams are now quietly meandering along their accustomed paths.

See Part 1 for further information about publications related to this event. These two drives are not intended to tell the entire story of Hurricane Camille. Every person has his own story and each area of the county its unique set of circumstances and difficulties.

TOTAL MILES: 32.3
FROM THE AMHERST CIRCLE:
Take Rt. 29 North to Lovingston (16.6 mi.).

MILES/DIRECTIONS	COMMENTARY
STARTING POINT Traffic light on Rt. 29 Turn right at the light onto Front Street, Rt. 29-Business.	In 1969, the Lovingston Rt. 29 bypass was being constructed; the newly-paved lanes served as a command center for gathering and disseminating information, for coordinating relief work, and as a landing strip for helicopters and small aircraft used in the search, rescue, and recovery effort. The use of the bypass in this manner even spawned a country song. The build-up of water rushing from a creek and the mountain above the town flooded Lovingston. Some of the town's buildings had deep water and mud running through the first floor.

0.8 Follow Front Street to its end (staying straight where an access to Rt. 29 bears left).	The Wells-Sheffield Funeral Home, on the right, served as the receiving station for the victims for identification. A refrigerated truck parked beside the funeral home was used to keep the bodies for this function.
1.0 Bear right on Orchard Street.	
1.1 Another right onto Court Street	The homes on Court Street received the impact of mudslides and water from the mountain above. Many homes suffered significant damage, such as flooded and mud-filled basements or collapsed walls. Those who witnessed the events spoke of the tremendous noise of the rockslides from the mountains.
1.5 Drive ahead to the Nelson County Courthouse, on left.	At the top of the steps leading to the courthouse grounds stands a monument to the victims of Hurricane Camille. The final toll is recorded as 84 identified fatalities, 33 known missing, and 8 never identified. The unidentified bodies eventually were taken to Richmond where they were cremated. The ashes and records remain there.
1.7 Turn right onto Main Street, cross Front Street (stop sign), and proceed to Rt. 29-N, Thomas Nelson Highway, and turn right.	At the intersection of Main Street and Rt. 29 was the headquarters, the "nerve center," of relief operations, and was manned by Virginia State Police, the Sheriff's Department staff, and volunteers.

3.2

Rt. 29-N, pass Rt. 641 (Eades Lane)

Eades Lane is of particular significance and should be noted as a landmark. From near this point, Colleen Thompson started her incredible experience as she was swept away from her family by the rushing water that night. Details of stories such as hers and others are chronicled in *Heartbeats of Nelson*.

Muddy Creek runs parallel to Rt. 29, on the right.

It has been stated that the amount of earth that the rainfall brought down in mudslides was the equivalent of 1000 years of erosion. The height of the storm was believed to have been around 3:00 a.m., when almost all electric service ceased, freezing the clocks at that hour.

For many years afterward, the mountains to the left showed bare scars, revealing areas where water, trees, and tons of earth crashed through the hollows to areas below. A few scars can still be seen, more visible in the winter, with the viewer's careful scrutiny.

7.1

Ridgecrest Baptist Church stands atop a hill, with Muddy Creek running behind it. It was behind this church that an exhausted Colleen Thompson concluded her dark but miraculous journey, as she caught some tree branches and pulled herself from the flood waters. She stayed there and was rescued that afternoon and taken by helicopter to the emergency room in Lynchburg, where she saw her son who had been evacuated earlier.

Several victims of the flood are buried in this church cemetery.

8.1

Davis Creek crosses under the road, joining Muddy Creek (on the right).

MILES/DIRECTIONS	COMMENTARY
8.7 Rt. 29 bridge over Rockfish River	Even though a tremendous flow of water rushed through this area, where Davis Creek and Muddy Creek ran into the Rockfish River, this bridge remained standing. Much debris was caught in the bridge structure, altering the course of the raging water and dispersing it over low-lying areas. This area is locally known as Woods Mill, so named for a mill of former times. Rainfall was reported to be in excess of 25 inches, although official measurement was virtually impossible. Records were circumstantial and anecdotal, but people reported an inability to breathe without a bucket worn upside-down on the head. It has been stated that the saturation of the air approached the greatest water concentration possible.
8.9 Nelson County Wayside	A Virginia historical marker denotes the events related to Hurricane Camille. This small wayside along the Rockfish River features picnic tables and toilet facility.
Leave the parking area, cross Rt. 29, and make a left turn into the southbound lane.	
9.8 Rt. 29-S, Thomas Nelson Highway. Turn right onto Rt. 776, Grape Lawn Drive. This turn is easy to miss.	Davis Creek, on the left, parallels this road.
10.0 Bear left as Grape Lawn Drive continues.	Rocky Road bears to the right. Grape Lawn continues to the left; it is gravel at this point.
11.0	Grape Lawn Drive crosses Davis Creek. A massive volume of water washed down the mountain via this route. Numerous fatalities occurred in the hollows above Davis Creek.

12.0

Grape Lawn Drive to
Rt. 623, Davis Creek
Road

Right turn onto Rt.
623

12.2
Turn right on the
gravel entry road for
the Oak Hill Baptist
Church Cemetery.

A walk through this small cemetery will be an
humbling experience, as many gravestones
reveal a number of names with date of death
as August 20, 1969 (some are marked only as
1969). These victims lived along Davis Creek and
its north fork which flowed down through the
hollows above this site.

Not all gravestones mark actual graves; some
represent those whose remains have never been
found. One extended family suffered 22 losses.

(Note: There are two Oak Hill Baptist Churches
in Nelson County, both have nearby cemeteries,
and both lost members to Hurricane Camille. The
other is in Massies Mill.)

Turn right out of Oak
Hill Cemetery and
proceed 1.9 mi. to
Perry Lane.

This part of the drive will lead to scenic roads
along the two forks of Davis Creek. Many of the
victims were living in this area.

Both Perry Lane and Davis Creek Road at this
point are gravel.

14.2
Turn right onto Perry
Lane

This road leads through the hollow with the
north fork of Davis Creek flowing quietly on the
left. Large boulders are visible along the creek;
many of these stones were deposited by the
raging waters in August, 1969.

16.1
A turn-around spot
is available here.
Retrace the route
back to Davis Creek
Road.

MILES/DIRECTIONS	COMMENTARY
18.0 Turn right and follow Rt. 623, Davis Creek Road, to its end.	This road follows Davis Creek through the hollow. At the end of this road ("End State Maintenance" sign) was a large apple orchard. As the earth recovered from the upheaval of Hurricane Camille and sprouted new growth, a seedling of an unknown variety of apple appeared. Named "Ginger Gold," it is now produced and marketed nationwide.
19.7 Turn around and follow Rt. 623, Davis Creek Road, bearing right at the paved surface, back to Rt. 29-S.	
24.4 Turn right onto U.S. 29-S. Stay on Rt. 29-S to "Oakland," the Museum of Nelson County History.	This concludes Part 2 of the Hurricane Camille tour.
32.3 **OPTIONAL STOP** To return to Amherst, turn right out of the parking lot onto Rt. 29-S, 13.4 miles.	"Oakland—The Museum of Nelson County History" houses a permanent exhibit and other information on Hurricane Camille. It is open Sat. (10:00 a.m. to 4:00 p.m.) and Sun. (1:00 to 4:00 p.m.) or by appointment. An admission fee is charged. PO Box 39, Lovingston VA 22949 Physical address: 5365 Thomas Nelson Highway Phone: 434-263-8400 www.oakland-museum.org oaklandmuseum@gmail.com